If I Can,
Y-Y-You Can!

If I Can,
Y-Y-You Can!

*Giving All You've Got
to Become All You Can Be*

NEAL JEFFREY

SAMPSON
PUBLISHING

If I Can, Y-Y-You Can! is published by:
SAMPSON PUBLISHING
A Division of Sampson Resources
4887 Alpha Road, Suite 220
Dallas, Texas 75244
800-371-5248
sampsonpublishing.com

ISBN-10: 0-615-31183-0
ISBN-13: 978-0-615-31183-8

Printed in the United States of America
2009

SPECIAL SALES
This book is available in special discounts when purchased in bulk quantities by churches, organizations, corporations, and special study groups. For information, contact the publisher at 800-371-5248 or at sampsonpublishing.com.

Contents

INTRODUCTION

Fired Up!

When I showed up for my very first high school football practice as a freshman, I already had six years of team football behind me. I started playing flag football in the third grade and continued with tackle football from the fourth grade on. That doesn't count all the backyard games I played with my buddies after school and on weekends. And when I couldn't get into a game somewhere, I spent hours alone at the schoolyard firing footballs at poles and trash cans to improve my aim.

All through my childhood years I had been looking forward to the day when I could play high school football. I was fired up about elevating my game to a new level where the action was faster, the competition was tougher, the pressure was greater and the cheerleaders were cuter. It was my chance to prove to the world – especially to the cheerleaders – that I was an awesome stud quarterback on my way to becoming a big star in college and professional football. So you can imagine how dumb I felt starting my career by racking up a bunch of penalties against my team. Here's how that happened.

In our high school games, the quarterback had twenty-five seconds to call a play in the huddle. In that time, I had to communicate three things to my teammates: the formation to line up in; the specific play I wanted to run; and the snap count for hiking the ball. If a QB couldn't get his team to the line of scrimmage and snap the ball in time, the referee threw a flag, blew the whistle, and penalized the team five yards for what's called "delay of game." Well, for me, twenty-five seconds just wasn't enough time! You see, I'm a stutterer. When I knelt in the huddle to call a play, I would often begin to stutter and couldn't get all the information out in twenty-five seconds. Needless to say, I was costing our team a ton of yardage, and I definitely wasn't impressing the cheerleaders or my coach.

So, Coach devised a system where I never had to say anything during the game. In fact, he said, "Jeffrey, you just kneel down in the huddle as usual and act like you're doing something. But don't open your mouth because it just confuses everybody!" He had our split end call the plays in the huddle. When we got to the line of scrimmage, our fullback – who always lined up right behind me – called out the signals: "Hut, hut, hut!" You should have seen the reaction from the other team at the start of each game. They could hear the "huts" coming from somewhere, but when they looked at me, I was just standing there behind the center smiling at them!

If you're thinking that my world as a kid revolved around football, you'd be right. Football has been a huge part of my life. After four years of high school football, I was privileged to play quarterback for Baylor University in Waco, Texas, for four years. I went on to play quarterback with the San Diego Chargers of the NFL for three years. I enjoyed a measure of success, collected a few trophies and now realize that the experience of playing football at every level impacted my life in many ways.

If you suspect that being a stutterer also made a huge impact on my life, you would be right again. Stuttering has been a constant presence and a nagging obstacle through my entire life and in everything I do. When I was a kid, I used to describe myself as a bad stutterer; but I soon realized that wasn't true. In reality, I'm a very good stutterer. I don't mean to brag, but if stuttering was a competitive sport, I'd probably have a shelf full of trophies for that, too! No question about it – being a stutterer has made a tremendous impact on my life.

As a kid, my stuttering affected everything I did. For example, when I answered the phone at home, sometimes I'd get stuck and couldn't get a word out. So I'd just hang up on people. In school, I sometimes had trouble saying "here" during roll call and got marked absent a lot. As a high school freshman I had to take a speech class. Our first assignment was to give a three-minute speech about ourselves in front of the class. That was a disaster. I stood in front of the class for about ten minutes without saying much of anything. My teacher, Mrs. Frazier, graciously let me sit down and gave me a B for effort. I've always been grateful to her for that. As a sophomore, I took a Spanish class. If you can imagine me stuttering in English, you should have heard me in Spanish!

Really, though, being a stutterer is no big deal – unless you want to say something. Then believe me, it is going to be a factor. I can honestly say that if stuttering has done anything for me, it has definitely made my life more exciting. I'm never sure in any situation if I will be able to say something or not. I've been in thousands of situations where I've had something I wanted to say and just had an exciting time trying to get it said.

Big Obstacles and Big Dreams

You may be wondering why a guy with a speech impediment would play quarterback. After all, he's the guy on the team who does the most talking during a game. It's a fair question, and here's the straight answer: *Because ever since I was a little kid, playing quarterback was my biggest dream.* I loved the great game of football, and I loved being the guy on the team who made things happen. I didn't want to play any other position. Deep down I knew I was born to play quarterback.

Living my big dream was so important that I was determined to get through anything that stood in the way of playing football, even my stuttering.

Remember that great movie *Chariots of Fire?* One of the main characters was Eric Liddell, a star rugby player and runner for Scotland during the early 1900s. In one scene he explains to his sister why he wants to train for the Olympics even though he is also preparing to be a missionary. Liddell's line in the film goes, "God made me for a purpose – for China. But He also made me *fast*. When I run, I feel His pleasure." That's just how I felt about football! I might have said Liddell's line like this: "God gave me a good arm and the mentality for playing quarterback. When I'm leading my team down the field for a touchdown, I feel His pleasure." Living my big dream was so important that I was determined to get through anything that stood in the way of playing football, even my stuttering.

I'm sure you have big dreams for your life. Everybody does. What are your dreams? What do you want to experience and achieve more than anything else? What brings you the most pleasure? What do you sense you are wired to do? In other words, if you borrowed Eric Liddell's line to describe your dreams, what would it sound like? Maybe you would say something like:

- "Ever since I ran my own lemonade stand as a kid, my dream has been to own my own business."
- "God gave me talent for art. When I draw or paint I feel His pleasure."
- "The thing that really fires me up is fixing stuff – computers, appliances, gadgets."
- "I'm a natural-born people person. I love being around and encouraging people."
- "I love helping people learn. I've always wanted to be a classroom teacher."
- "I want our company to produce such outstanding products that we will one day be ranked the leader in our field."

Having big dreams is good and natural. Your dreams have a way of revealing how God wired you. They represent the real you *inside* yearning to be expressed in the real world *outside*. The Bible says, "A desire accomplished is sweet to the soul" (Proverbs 13:19). Pursuing and living your big dreams and deep desires is one way to worship and praise the God who created you.

But don't think it will be easy. Like me, you will have to get through the challenges that stand between you and your dreams. Former college football coach Lou Holtz said, "Show me someone who has done something worthwhile, and I'll show you someone who has overcome adversity." Your adversity may not be stuttering, but everybody has shortcomings, weaknesses and limitations. Everybody has to deal with doubts and fears and the temptation to quit or settle for less than the best. Everybody gets knocked down every now and then by negative circumstances.

Whatever defeats or disabilities you face, achieving your big dreams is worth whatever it takes to overcome them. And I'm here to tell you that you can do it! I mean, if I could do what I did on the football field as a stutterer, you can overcome your doubts and knock-downs to realize your dreams. Believe me, there is nothing special or extraordinary about me. I'm just "regular people" like you with a lot of stuff to get through in order to reach my dreams and live out my God-given purpose. In fact, I wrote this book to inspire and encourage you on your journey to achieving your dreams.

What I want you to realize is that God created you for a special purpose. He wants to do incredible things in you and through you that will inspire and help others; and He will use everything that happens in your life – the good, the bad, and the ugly – to accomplish that purpose. That's why I'm so excited to share my story with you, because if God can do anything worthwhile in me, He can do the same thing in you. In other words, if I can, y-y-you can!

Called to a Purpose

I've already mentioned that football and stuttering are two huge, life-shaping parts of my story, and in the pages ahead I'll tell you more about how a guy who couldn't even call plays in the huddle made it to the NFL. But there's another thing that is bigger than that. It has to do with my calling in life. Again, I can see myself in *Chariots of Fire*. Eric Liddell's dream was to run, and run he did – winning a gold medal at the 1924 Olympic Games in Paris! But as a young man committed to serving God, Liddell's calling was to be a missionary to China. His line in the movie is, "God made me for a purpose – for China."

Shortly after winning his gold medal, Liddell left Scotland for China, and served there until his death.

Like Eric Liddell, I knew from my high school days that God had something more important for me to do than just play football. Growing up, I always admired pastors, evangelists, motivational speakers and great Christian athletes who could preach and teach the Bible. My life had been changed as God spoke to me through these people. As a teenager I used to think, "Man, wouldn't it be awesome to be used by God that way?" Then I began to hear God say to me, "Neal, I *do* want to use you that way, and it will be *awesome!*"

If you've had a hard time believing that a stutterer could be an NFL quarterback, what do you think about a stutterer becoming a preacher and professional speaker? Well, just multiply your doubts by about a gazillion, and you'll have an idea how I felt. My first response was, "God, stutterers don't make good preachers, so there's no way that can happen for me!" But even while playing football in college and the NFL, God was moving me in His direction for my life. I was involved in a great organization called Fellowship of Christian Athletes, which gave me opportunities to share my faith through public speaking. Soon I felt led to begin taking seminary courses during the off-season and working toward a divinity degree.

After my third season with the Chargers, I reached a fork in the road. I probably could have stayed in the NFL for several more years as a backup quarterback, but I was increasingly drawn toward God's call on my life. Finally, I hung up the cleats at the end of my third pro season and returned to seminary to complete my graduate degree.

For more than twenty-five years now, I have been associate pastor at the Prestonwood Baptist Church in Plano, Texas. I do all the things that pastors do: preach sermons, lead Bible studies, counsel people with problems, visit sick people and conduct weddings and funerals. I also do a lot of speaking at other churches, conferences and corporate meetings. And, yes, I'm still a world-class stutterer! I really enjoyed those years of playing football and just had some great experiences on and off the field! I'll talk about some of them in this book. But there is no amount of touchdowns or victories or championships that can match the thrill of *being* what God created me to be and *doing* what He created me to do.

Let me ask you a couple of questions on the subject of God's plans for you. The first question is – have you discovered what God has called you to be and to do in life? I'm not saying God wants you to be a speaker like me or a missionary like Eric Liddell. God may lead you to be a mechanic or a teacher or a computer tech or a writer or a foster parent or a politician or even a professional athlete who serves God faithfully. His greatest and highest calling for you might be as a devoted wife and stay-at-home mom. Nothing could be greater! The point is: God has a plan for you that just might be more incredible than your wildest dreams.

> ❖
>
> *...there is no amount of touchdowns or victories or championships that can match the thrill of **being** what God created me to be and **doing** what He created me to do.*
>
> ❖

The second question is – what's keeping you from being what God wants you to be? I'm talking about anything and everything that causes you to say things like, "I can't do it" or "I'm not qualified" or "Who me? You've got to be kidding!" I'm talking about what you may view as feelings of inadequacy, character defects or disabilities or disadvantages. And I'm talking about the knock-downs, disappointments and defeats that have caused you to give up time and time again. Life's greatest challenge is saying yes to what God has called you to do despite all your reasons to say no. And life's greatest reward is seeing what God does in response to your yes.

Here's my point: *If God can use a stuttering old jock like me to make a positive impact on the world, he can do amazing things through you no matter what odds seem to be stacked against you.* I know from personal experience that God can do the improbable and the impossible for anyone. He can get you through your impossible challenges, help you realize your improbable dreams, and make a mark of significance on your world that will last forever. I've written this book to help you get fired up about finding and fulfilling God's very best, no matter what you have to go through.

Fired Up to Live Large

Some of my greatest experiences as a football player happened before the game ever started. If you've ever played a team sport, you know what I mean. You're sitting there in the locker room with your teammates – suited up, warmed up and chomping at the bit to get it on! Then the coach walks in and gives a pep talk. He or she reminds you of some things you already know, adds a few things you hadn't thought about, then says something dynamic and powerful that makes you want to play like you've never played before.

Pep talks fired me up so much as an athlete that I love giving pep talks to athletes today! Many years ago I gave a pep talk to the Baylor University football team before a big game against the University of Nebraska, an awesome football powerhouse during those years. Baylor was a 35-point underdog to the Cornhuskers that day, so it was my job to fire up the team to play their best. In all humility, I can honestly say that I gave the greatest pep talk that day I think I've ever heard! I mean I pumped them up, I fired them up, and I inspired them! By the end of my talk the guys were foaming at the mouth and ready to bust up the furniture! Well, our boys got beat that day 49-0. But I'm convinced if I hadn't given that great talk, we'd have gotten beat 100-0!

I've discovered that everybody gets something good out of a pep talk. We all face situations of overwhelming odds and need encouragement and inspiration to get through tough stuff. Even now you may be facing the challenge of your life, something that stands in your way like a flashing blockade or is chasing you like a silent monster. Or maybe you're just living under a cloud of the blahs or the blues. Whatever you're facing in life, you will benefit from a good pep talk that helps get you jumpstarted and challenged to plow through the stuff that is keeping you from your dreams and God's plans. I'm writing to encourage you and inspire you! I want you to meet your challenges head-on and pursue your dreams with all you've got.

I've been giving inspirational and motivational talks for nearly thirty years in business conventions and Bible studies, corporate sales conferences, sports teams, church retreats, youth meetings and church pulpits. I talk to men, women and students just like you who want to overcome great obstacles, accomplish great feats and live meaningful, significant lives. Like the coaches and teachers and mentors who fired you up as a kid, in this book I'm going to remind you of some important things you already know; I'll share a few things you may not have thought about, and I'll challenge you to experience God's best for your life today. I want to fire you up!

Higher, Swifter, Stronger

Three Latin words make up what may be the shortest and oldest pep talk in history. The words are *altius, citius, fortius,* the motto of the Olympic Games. Simply translated, they mean *higher, swifter, stronger.* This motto has challenged some of the greatest athletes in history and continues to challenge athletes all over the world by saying, "Hey, no matter how high they jumped in the past, *we* will jump higher! No matter how fast they ran in the past, *we* will run faster! No matter how strong they were in the past, *we* will be stronger!"

The Olympic motto is the opposite of the more familiar Latin phrase *status quo,* which means *the way things are,* or as Ronald Reagan once said, "status quo is Latin for 'the mess we're in.'" Nobody runs faster, leaps higher or lifts stronger when they settle for the status quo. Count on it: If you're content with life as usual, you'll probably never make the team's starting lineup, your golf swing will never get straightened out, you won't lose the weight you want to lose, and you'll be stuck in your dead-end job until you're dead.

> *Whether you're teen-aged, middle-aged, or senior-aged, you know there's much more to who you are and what you can do than the world has seen so far.*

The Olympic motto fires me up to leave the status quo behind, to tackle the mountains and monsters in my life head-on, and press on to be higher, swifter and stronger in every way. I want to make the most of every opportunity and experience everything God has for me, and I have a hunch that you want the same. No matter what you may have achieved up to this point in life, hopefully you would say that you haven't yet peaked – there's still something left. Whether you're teen-aged, middle-aged, or senior-aged, you know there's much more to who you are and what you can do than the world has seen so far. You yearn to break free of the stuff holding you back so you can accomplish more, achieve more, and make a significant difference in the world with the one and only life you have to live.

I'm convinced that the key to getting past your difficulties and living the life God has for you is to think and respond the right way in six critical areas. In fact, each major section of this book focuses on one of these areas.

The first critical area is how you view and value your time. Let's face it: Each of us has a limited number of years, months, weeks and days to live. Even more sobering is the reality that none of us knows how much time we have left. Every day of your life is precious. That's why it's important to make the most of every single day you're privileged to wake up.

The second critical area is how you view and value your dreams and destiny. Everything in life starts with a dream. Great things happen when people dream what could be, seek God's best plans for their lives, and then believe and work hard to turn those dreams and plans into reality. You can get through a mountain of problems if you have a great dream propelling you toward your destiny.

The third critical area is how you view and value the negatives in your life. God wants to use the very things you consider obstacles or difficulties to accomplish His great plans for you. He is all about turning tears of disappointment and defeat into the satisfaction of victory. Your life will change when you embrace a positive attitude toward the negatives you face.

The fourth critical area is how you view and value doing the right thing. There's a war going on between what God wants to do in your life and the negatives that can hold you back. In order to get past the negatives and achieve God's great dreams, you will have to battle an enemy who has vowed to destroy everything right and good that God has for you.

The fifth critical area is how you view and value the power of belief. When someone who believes shows up in a situation, things change for the better.

The power of your belief makes all the difference in getting you through your disappointments and defeats. Your beliefs and how you demonstrate them are indispensible in achieving your great dreams and experiencing God's incredible plans.

The sixth critical area is how you view and value the power of love. Love is the greatest motivating force in the world. People who know that they are loved just for who they are – even with their weaknesses and faults – cannot be stopped in whatever they set out to do. Tapping into the power of love is an important key to dealing with the negatives in life and achieving your dreams.

If you are ready to leave the status quo behind and set out on the great adventure of experiencing your best life ever, I can help you get started! You're going to be challenged to move ahead with your dreams no matter what is holding you back. You're going to experience the excitement of living your life as God meant it to be lived. You're going to find out firsthand what's it's like to go beyond the "ho-hum" of the status quo to the "oh, yeah" of higher, swifter, stronger.

The time clock is ticking, so let's not waste another minute. Turn the page and tackle the first critical area: your time.

I

EVERY DAY COUNTS
How to View and Value Your Time

Teach us to number our days, that we may gain a heart of wisdom.
PSALM 90:12

*The greatest waste in all of our earth, which cannot be recycled
or reclaimed, is our waste of the time that God has given each of us.*
BILLY GRAHAM

1

Life Comes with a "Use By" Date

Eighteen years seems like a long time to play football – starting with flag football in the third grade and ending after three years with the San Diego Chargers of the National Football League. That's a lot of games, a lot of practices, a lot of drills, a lot of running and a lot of pain. It's hard to imagine how many times I drew back my right arm and threw a football during those years, but I'll bet I did it hundreds of thousands of times. And loved every minute of it!

But you know what? Today those eighteen years seem like the blink of an eye. You see – my football days are over. They're long gone. I had a brief window of time as a young man to play a great game, but that window has closed for me, and I'll never play football competitively again. Do I miss it? You bet, especially on Friday nights. Where I live, high school football is huge. There's nothing like being up in the stands, taking in all the sights and sounds and smells, watching two good teams play their hearts out. I love it! And when I'm watching the game I love, something tugs at my insides like a riptide, and I would give almost anything to be able to go back there and do it all again! But I've had my shot, and I'll never get another one.

Here's the point: *You only have so much time in life. That's why every day is precious!* Dallas Cowboys' coach Tom Landry used to say, "Today, you have

21

100 percent of your life left." But that 100 percent is different for everybody. We all want to believe that we have many decades of good health and productivity ahead of us, but the reality is that my 100 percent or your 100 percent may mean only a few years, a few months or a few days. That 100 percent ended too quickly for Tom Landry. The Bible refers to our life as "a mist that appears for a little while and then vanishes" (James 4:14 NIV). Only God knows our expiration date. That's why it's important to make the most of the days we have left.

Only God knows our expiration date. That's why it's important to make the most of the days we have left.

Every day, every month, every year you're alive is nothing less than a precious gift from God. This gift is not yours to set on a shelf and enjoy like you would a gun rack full of rifles and shotguns or a buffet loaded with antique china. God's gift of time is something He intends for you to use for noble purposes. The Bible stresses the importance of "redeeming the time" (Ephesians 5:16). The word "redeeming" can be translated "rescuing." Just imagine a river of time constantly flowing past you. Those minutes and hours and days need to be rescued – pulled from the water – and put to good use before they disappear downstream forever. God is the one who decides how much time we have to use, but He puts into our hands the responsibility for making the most of the opportunities that come along with it.

For example, let's say you're a mom whose kids are out of the nest, and you've got time on your hands. You've you been thinking for months about volunteering at a homeless women's shelter in your community, at a nearby hospital or at your church. Listen, valuable time is slipping away. Make a phone call and get started today!

Perhaps you're a student who has noticed a new kid in class who could use a little attention and friendship from somebody. What's keeping you from finding that kid at lunchtime and introducing yourself? Other kids won't have anything to do with him, but other kids aren't *you*. Don't lose another day. Do it!

Maybe you have a business colleague whose behavior is hurting his family.

You don't know exactly what to say, so you've been putting off saying anything at all. The situation is getting worse every day. Set up a lunch date with him as soon as possible and share your concern. What's to lose? Maybe his family and career – if you don't help him.

Every day is precious, so make the most of the minutes and hours you have been given.

A Brief Window of Time

I've often thought about what I would do differently if I could start over as an athlete. I'll tell you what I'd do: I would be more committed to making the most of my all-too-short window of opportunity. I worked hard as a football player, but I would work harder now. I'd run an extra lap or two at every practice. I'd do a few more reps in the weight room. I'd spend more time studying game films. I'd push myself toward greater excellence.

So many of the athletes I see today take the path of least resistance instead of the path of maximum excellence. They love being on a team – getting the attention, feeling the pride of wearing the uniform, hearing the cheers of the crowd – but they're not too excited about doing what it takes to play at that "excellence" level. King Solomon wisely wrote, "Whatever your hand finds to do, do it with your might" (Ecclesiastes 9:10). That word "might" can also be translated "force." If Solomon were writing to athletes today, he might say, "Whatever you decide to play, put some *force* behind it, push yourself, get the most out of it – drive, excel! Go higher, swifter, stronger!"

Most athletes love their sport and plan to get more committed and be the best they can be. The problem is that many of them settle into the comfort zone of just getting by. They essentially start loafing. But it's not a real "loaf," because if their loafing was very obvious they'd be kicked off the team. So these athletes settle for being members of the team without it costing them too much or interrupting their social life and other activities. In other words, they opt for the status quo instead of higher, swifter, stronger.

John C. Maxwell writes, "Too many talented people who start with an advantage over others lose that advantage because they *rest* on their talent instead of *raising* their talent." One of the saddest things I can imagine is talented athletes who refuse to develop and use the gifts God has given them. Their approach is to just "get by." They fail to realize that every drill, every practice, every game and every season is an opportunity to get better and better. The tragedy is that these athletes reach the end of their playing careers and realize they have missed it! Instead of feeling satisfied and fulfilled, they walk away under a nagging shadow of regret over what might have been, what they could have achieved if only they'd made the most of that window of time.

Days of Unlimited Excellence

Athletes who fail to give their best illustrate another key point about the time available to us: The number of our days on earth is in God's hands, but the excellence of our activity during those days is in our hands. What is excellence anyway? Excellence is a state of high quality or superiority. We're not talking about perfection, because that's beyond our grasp. NBA coach Pat Riley said, "Excellence is the gradual result of always striving to do better." Excellence is what happens when you continue striving to go higher, swifter, stronger.

Athletes in pursuit of excellence make every opportunity count – every play, every practice, every game and every season – as if it might be their last. They are determined not to waste a single opportunity to improve and excel because they know it will greatly affect the quality of their career. The pursuit of excellence will make a huge impact on your life when it comes to getting through the negatives you face in order to make the most of the life God has given you.

❖

The number of our days on earth is in God's hands, but the excellence of our activity during those days is in our hands.

❖

Jesus told a parable in Matthew 25:13-40 that gives us a good contrast between the excellence of higher, swifter, stronger and the status quo of settling for less than our best. It's the story of a rich landowner who was preparing to leave on a long journey. He gave his three servants five talents, three talents, and one talent respectively, "each according to his own ability" (Matt. 25:15). A "talent" of gold in New Testament times would be worth around a million dollars or more in today's value. The servants were responsible for investing the talents given to them while the master was away. The parable tells us that the first two servants got right to work investing their talent and doubled it, while the third servant simply buried his talent in the ground. When the master returned, he praised and rewarded the first two servants for their efforts. But he called the third servant "wicked and lazy" (Matt. 25:26) and fired him on the spot.

There are three lessons about excellence for us in this story. *First, we don't all have the same God-given abilities and resources.* The three servants were given different amounts to invest based on their different abilities. In a similar way, you may have a great singing voice, while someone else can't carry a tune if it had handles. One person may be a whiz at numbers, while another can't balance a checkbook. The point is that while nobody excels at everything, each of us can excel at something.

Second, we don't all experience the same results and rewards from investing our abilities and resources. The first two servants reaped different profits, and their rewards from the master were different. The bottom line is that everyone who invests his or her gifts and resources for the Master will experience results and rewards even though they may be different.

Third, we all have the same opportunity to live for excellence no matter what we have or how we may profit. Just like the three servants, the issue isn't how much we have to work with, but how we work with what we have. If you commit to filling your days pursuing excellence in how you live, you can look forward to the same praise the two faithful servants received: "Well done, good and faithful servant" (Matt. 25:21).

All of us are tempted to choose the path of least resistance when it comes to the opportunities we encounter in life. Instead of giving life all we've got and pushing ourselves to go higher, swifter and stronger, we start coasting. It happens when we stop stretching, striving and pushing ourselves toward excellence in what we do. The real tragedy of coasting or settling for the status quo comes at the end of our lives. We look back with regret, realizing that we settled for less than the maximum investment of our gifts and abilities, and squandered the time and opportunities God gave us.

Rescuing Minutes One by One

There are only so many hours and minutes in the day. How can you decide the best way to use them? Here are five encouraging tips.

1. Take care of what's close by. When the great prophet Nehemiah set out to rebuild the broken-down walls of Jerusalem, he instructed each Israelite family to work on the section of the wall closest to where they lived. That's good advice for us today. Use your precious time to impact those things closest to you – the most pressing needs of your family, your friends, your church, your community, and your own soul's well-being. As more windows of time open up, you can expand that circle to other tasks.

2. Tackle the tough stuff. Admit it: There are some things you'd rather put off indefinitely. Some responsibilities are just more pleasant than others. So, I suggest picking one tough job each day to get out of the way before moving on to what you would really rather do.

3. Say it with me: "No!" There's an old Chinese proverb that says, "One cannot manage too many affairs: like pumpkins in the water, one pops up while you try to hold the other down." Somebody else said it this way: "To do two things at once is to do neither." Using precious time wisely means we must make choices, and sometimes that means saying no to some things in order to say yes to more important things.

4. Stick with the plan. If you let your busy days take control, you will be running from one need or hotspot to another. But if you take control of your busy days and manage them well, you will make the best use of every minute.

5. Don't worry, be happy! When you get to the end of each day, don't gripe and grumble about what you didn't get done. Instead, rejoice and be happy about the minutes you were able to rescue and use for good purposes.

The following lines from an unknown author bring a healthy wake-up call encouraging us to use our time wisely. You might want to copy these words and put them where you will see them every morning.

> This is the beginning of a new day.
> God has given me this day to use as I will.
> I can waste it or use it for good.
> What I do today is important because
> I am exchanging a day of my life for it.
> When tomorrow comes,
> this day will be gone forever,
> leaving in its place something
> that I have traded for it.
> I want it to be gain, not loss;
> good not evil; success not failure;
> in order that I shall not regret
> the price I paid for it.

Next, we'll talk about some of the best ways I know to make the most of every day God gives you.

2

Every Time Can Be the Best Time

It didn't take long for Phil Connors to realize that something really weird was going on. When he walked out of his hotel room on the morning of February 3, he walked into a major case of déjà vu. Everywhere he went, the same people he saw yesterday were doing the same things at the same times and in the same ways as yesterday. Connors thought he was going nuts! Finally, it dawned on him: It wasn't February 3 after all. It was February 2 – Groundhog Day – all over again.

Do you remember that movie from the early 1990s? A TV weatherman is sent to Punxsutawney, Pennsylvania, to do a Groundhog Day story; but when he wakes up the next morning – and every other morning for weeks – the very same day starts over. And he's the only character in the movie who knows that each new day is simply another rerun of February 2.

Once he figures out what's going on, the wily weatherman takes full advantage of his bizarre situation. After all, since he gets a "do-over" every single day, he doesn't have to worry about the long-term consequences of his actions. So he lives selfishly every day. He doesn't care about hurting people or disobeying the law because he knows he will wake up the next day with a clean slate. Eventually, however, he realizes that his self-centered approach to life is wrong, and he starts using each new February 2 to correct his wrongs and make a positive difference in people's lives.

Can you imagine the possibilities of having "do-over days" like that TV weatherman in the movie? For example, maybe you have a day when you foul everything up big-time – say something that hurts someone dear to you, accidently set the house on fire, run over the family dog, or whatever! Wouldn't it be great to have another chance or two to do that day over?

Well, it just won't happen. God gives everyone a limited number of days to use, and every one of them is fresh, new and full of promise. No reruns or do-over days. Whether you have a day of sky-high success or one of those dismal days of wasted opportunities, when it's over, it's over. You don't get to do it again. But here's the good news: Every new day you live you get to start with a clean slate – a brand new day ready to be used. I like how fitness expert Kim Lyons put it: "Yesterday is a cancelled check; tomorrow is a promissory note; today is the only cash you have – so spend it wisely."

Tackle Your Opportunities Today

During your lifetime, everything you do has a *first* attached to it: your first step, your first day at school, first date, first job, first driver's license, first time you say "I love you." But as you get older, you will eventually do everything for the *last* time – work your last day before retirement, buy your last car, watch your last cooking show on TV. And finally, your heart will beat one last time. You will draw your last breath, and your family will book your last accommodations – in the cemetery.

Here's what I'm saying: *You have only so many days to leave a positive mark. That's why every day is so precious. Don't miss a day or an opportunity. Leave that mark today!*

There haven't been many basketball players like "Pistol Pete" Maravich. This guy was incredible! As a star at Louisiana State University during the late 1960s, Maravich was a three-time All-American. He went on to play ten years in the NBA before a leg injury and alcoholism put an end to his career. In 1987,

Maravich was elected to the NBA Hall of Fame.

After a couple of years of searching for meaning in life, the retired hoop star became a Christian and began sharing his newfound faith wherever he had the opportunity. One of those opportunities came from Dr. James Dobson, who invited Maravich to be a guest on his radio program. Maravich flew to California from his home in Louisiana to be interviewed on *Focus on the Family*.

A few hours before the taping, Maravich and Dr. Dobson and some other guys got together for a pick-up basketball game at a nearby gym. They were catching their breath after the game when somebody asked Pete how it felt to be on the court again. The forty-year-old Maravich answered, "I feel great!" Two minutes later he dropped dead. Right there on the basketball court. An autopsy revealed that a rare, undetected heart defect had killed him. Maravich had no clue that the heart of a basketball star had been a ticking time bomb in his chest for his whole life.

Moments before his death, Pete Maravich had no idea that he had said "I love you" to his wife Jackie and two young sons for the last time. He didn't know he had shared his faith in Christ for the last time, read his Bible for the last time, prayed to his Father for the last time, taken his shot for the last time. I sure hope I have more warning than Pete Maravich did before my last day comes around. But the truth is, we never know for sure how many days we have left. So it's important to make every day count.

God's calendar for each of our lives has a last page and a final date, but that calendar is kept somewhere in heaven out of our reach. What we need to do is to live each day as if it is our last. Someone has said that yesterday is history, tomorrow is a mystery and today is a gift – I say unwrap it as you would a treasured present and use it! You don't know if you will wake up tomorrow, but you do have today. Do everything you are able to do today!

First Time, Last Time

On August 3, 1980, I discovered why God created me with shoulders. That's the day my wife Sheila and I welcomed our first child, Natalie Marie Jeffrey, into the world. Minutes after Natalie was delivered, the doctor wrapped her in a blanket and handed the little bundle to me. She fit perfectly on my shoulder! I loved holding her there, singing to her and rocking her to sleep during those first several months. Those were some of the most incredible times of my life. But I snuggled Natalie on my shoulder for the last time almost thirty years ago. Again, the point is this: you only have so many nights to snuggle the baby on your shoulder, so don't miss snuggling that baby tonight!

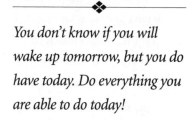

You don't know if you will wake up tomorrow, but you do have today. Do everything you are able to do today!

Sheila and I also have a daughter named Melissa and a son named James. When James was a little guy, he always wanted to play ball. Anytime he was throwing, catching or hitting something he was happy. Some days I actually thought I was too busy to play ball with James. I finally realized that one day he would be too busy to play ball with me, and one day I would be too old to throw, catch or hit a ball at all. Let me tell you, you have only so many days to play with your kids, so don't miss playing with them today! You'll probably get more out of it than they will.

One day you will tell your parents, husband or wife, or dear friends "I love you" for the last time. Today could be that day, your last chance to tell that special person how much he or she means to you and has enriched your life. Don't waste an opportunity. Your "I love you" needs to be said today, and it needs to be said with passion and feeling so that your loved ones hear it with their ears and feel it in their souls.

One day you will have your last opportunity to tell your coworkers, neighbors or fellow students about what Jesus has done in your life and what He can do in theirs. The people you take for granted every day can be transferred, move away, get sick, die or otherwise walk out of your life. The people in your sphere of influence need to hear the good news that God loves them – *today!*

One day you'll have your last chance to pray for people who need God's strength to make it through challenging times. One day you will have your last opportunity to give of your time and resources to serve the poor, the homeless, the abused, the neglected and the oppressed. The hurting people around you need your help – *today*!

One day you will find that the opportunity to bring healing to a relationship that seems to have withered and died is gone. You have been meaning to make things right with a church member you have wronged or a relative who won't speak to you or a child you're in conflict with. Any collapsing bridges that are keeping you at a distance from others need to be rebuilt – *today*!

Tasks Worth Your Time

If something is worth doing, it's usually worth doing today. A famous multimillionaire once said, "One worthwhile task carried to a successful conclusion is worth half-a-hundred half-finished tasks." But what kinds of things are really worthwhile? Philippians 4:8 gives us a number of ways to evaluate the many activities that demand our time and attention each day: "Finally, brethren, whatever things are true, whatever things are noble, whatever things are just, whatever things are pure, whatever things are lovely, whatever things are of good report, if there is any virtue and if there is anything praiseworthy – meditate on these things." Here are eight worthy things in which we should invest our time every day.

*Whatever things are **true**.* Investing your valuable time to advance the truth is worthwhile. For example, the time you personally invest in teaching your kids the importance of telling the truth, confronting local or national leaders who try to cover the truth, or being truthful in all your financial dealings – including tax returns – is time and effort well spent.

*Whatever things are **noble**.* The word "noble" refers to being honorable and principled. There's a saying that goes, "You've got to stand for something or you'll fall for anything." Your activities are worth your time if they help accomplish the honorable principles and causes you stand for – serving at your church, taking toys and clothing to orphanages, bringing at-risk children to vacation Bible school, coaching a children's sports team.

*Whatever things are **just**.* It's real easy to see what's wrong and needs to be fixed in your town, in your church, in your own family and even in yourself. It's quite another thing to roll up your sleeves and spend time doing whatever it takes to make things right and just.

*Whatever things are **pure**.* Purity refers to being morally clean and innocent. You may not be able singlehandedly to rid the world of all its moral evils, but you can take a stand against impurity where you live – in your community, your school, your household, your personal life.

*Whatever things are **lovely**.* Everybody enjoys things that are well-appointed, pleasing and lovely. Whether you're arranging flowers for the family dinner table, helping clean up an elderly neighbor's yard, texting encouragement or appreciation to a friend, or pointing out a spectacular sunset to your kids, investing your time doing things that are lovely is worthwhile.

*Whatever things are of **good report**.* The reference here is to things that are admirable or well-spoken of. Admirable activities prompt people to say things like "Fantastic!" or "That was great!" or "I can't tell you how good it made me feel to see that!" or "How inspiring!" It's all about doing things that fill a need and bless a heart.

*Whatever things are **virtuous**.* This word carries the meaning of moral excellence, strength and courage, a high standard for what is right. Whatever you do, this may be the last time you do it; so aim for those things that are virtuous.

*Whatever things are **praiseworthy**.* What better reason can there be for doing something than knowing it will bring praise to God? That's the ultimate goal of living with passion and excellence in everything you do. If God receives praise for it, you know your time and effort were well spent.

❖

Yesterday is in the disposal and tomorrow is still in the oven, so the only time you have to work with is today.

❖

Here's the key idea: Yesterday is in the disposal and tomorrow is still in the oven, so the only time you have to work with is today. Your life is the sum total of how you live today, so choose to master today!

Your Time Has Come

In Shakespeare's play *Julius Caesar*, Brutus kills Caesar, and he and his friend Cassius are running away. Back in town, Marc Antony stands up and makes his big speech and gets everybody on his side; then he and his friends go in hot pursuit of Brutus and Cassius. The scene is Brutus' campsite where he and Cassius are talking. They agree, "We can't run from this thing anymore; we have to stand and fight." So in Act 4, Scene 3, Brutus makes a classic statement:

> There is a tide in the affairs of men,
> Which, taken at the flood, leads on to fortune;
> Omitted, all the voyage of their life
> Is bound in shallows and in miseries.

Brutus knew it was their time to take a stand. It was their time to "catch the wave."

Now if you've ever been surfing, you know what it's like to be standing waist-deep in the surf looking for the big waves you're hoping to catch. You can see them forming out there, and in your mind you pick one out and think, "That's the one I'm going to get." As it gets closer, you can feel it building around you and see it curling almost on top of you. You know that if you hit that wave just right, you will ride that thing all the way to the beach. It's going to be a rush – indescribable, awesome! But you also know that if you miss it, you'll be "in the shallows and miseries" again where nothing is happening.

Here's what I want to stress: Today is your day to catch the wave. Today is your opportunity to make a worthwhile mark that cannot be erased. This is *your* time!

Think about some of the major characters of the Bible: Abraham, Moses, David, Esther, Mary the mother of Jesus, Peter and Paul. God did incredible things through them. They caught the wave and great things happened. But these patriarchs and kings and apostles and saints are gone now. They had their time and blessed us with their experiences and writings, but they are gone. Now it's *your* time!

Consider the godly men and women of history who paved the way for our faith to take root: people like Martin Luther, William Tyndale, John Wycliffe, Hudson Taylor and Billy Graham. They made the most of their time. This is *your* time. What are you going to do with it? Mother Teresa dedicated the last forty-five years of her life living in the slums of the world caring for the poor. At her death in 1997, she left over 600 active missions in more than 100 countries. She caught the wave and used her time to relieve great human need. But Mother Teresa is gone. Now it's *your* time to touch the lives of hurting people!

Closer to home, it's *your* time to love your husband or wife the way God intended for them to be loved. And they desperately want to be loved. As a young person, it's *your* time to honor and respect your parents as God's instruments for shaping your life. Parent, it's *your* time to nurture and protect your kids and cut a path of excellence for them to follow. It's *your* time to live with integrity and reliability among those with whom you work or go to school. Wherever you go and whatever you do, it's *your* time to make a difference, to touch a life, to be an example and to leave a positive mark that will be remembered after you're gone. Will you start making the most of *your* time – today?

3

Just One Thing

There's a great scene in the classic comedy film *City Slickers* that illustrates the importance of focusing your life on what's most important. Mitch, a city slicker played by Billy Crystal, is riding the range and rounding up strays with a tough-as-nails old cowboy named Curly, played by the late Jack Palance. Approaching his fortieth birthday, Mitch is struggling through a midlife crisis in his job and marriage.

As they ride along, Curly talks about how great cowboy life is. Mitch says, "That's great. Your life makes sense to you."

"You city folk," Curly says. "You all come up here around the same age with the same problems. Spend about fifty weeks getting knots in your rope, and then you think two weeks up here will untie them for you. None of you get it."

Curly continues, "Do you know what the secret of life is?"

Mitch answers eagerly, "No. What?"

"This," Curly says, raising his index finger.

Mitch looks puzzled. "Your finger?"

"One thing, just one thing," Curly explains, finger still up. "You stick to that and everything else don't mean nothing."

"That's great, but what's the 'one thing'?" Mitch says, lifting his finger.

Curly smiles as he lowers his finger to point directly at Mitch and says, "That's what you've got to figure out."

The *Real* One Thing

The Bible is the best place to find out what that "one thing" really is. It's not one thing among many equal things. It's not *your* one thing or *my* one thing, as if everybody can choose the one thing that works best for him or her. It's *THE* one thing, *God's* one thing for us that makes all the difference in how our days on earth count. The Apostle Paul provides a crystal clear summary in Colossians 1:15-18 of what God's one thing is. Since all the pronouns in these verses refer to Jesus Christ, I have substituted the name *Jesus* for each of them.

> *Jesus is the image of the invisible God, the firstborn over all creation. For by Jesus all things were created that are in heaven and that are on earth, visible and invisible, whether thrones or dominions or principalities or powers. All things were created through Jesus and for Jesus. And Jesus is before all things, and in Jesus all things consist. And Jesus is the head of the body, the church, who is the beginning, the firstborn from the dead, that in all things Jesus may have the preeminence.* (Colossians 1:15-18)

What qualifies Jesus to be the one main thing in your life? I see six answers in these verses.

First, *Jesus is the invisible God who came to earth in visible form* (Col. 1:15). Jesus told his disciples, "He who has seen me has seen the Father" (John 14:9). Jesus is God, and God is *the* one main thing.

Second, *Jesus created the world and everything in it* (Col. 1:16). If it were not for Jesus, you wouldn't even be here. That kind of puts Him at the center of things, wouldn't you say?

Third, *everything was created by Jesus and for Jesus* (Col. 1:16). Think about it: the reason you were created in the first place was for Jesus. If you are living outside a personal relationship with Jesus Christ, you're not living out your reason for being here.

Fourth, *Jesus holds everything together* (Col. 1:17). He is the invisible force that keeps the largest heavenly bodies and the tiniest subatomic particles in place.

Fifth, *Jesus is King over all who will be in heaven for eternity* (Col. 1:18). If you want to live forever, you must acknowledge Jesus as Lord. Anyone who doesn't confess him as Lord will not live with Him in heaven.

Sixth, *Jesus is number one in everything* (Col. 1:18). The word in the verse is "preeminence," which means supreme, primary, dominant and incomparable. Jesus owns first place in everything – always has, does, always will. He alone is the *one* thing.

Jesus Christ alone is great enough to shape your life for making a positive impact on the people around you and leaving a lasting mark of significance on your world. And He alone is able to get you through all the disappointments, defeats and heartaches you will experience along your journey through life. Jesus must be elevated to His rightful place far above all other admired and important things. As the old saying goes, "If Jesus isn't Lord *of* all, He isn't Lord *at* all."

Is Football Enough?

For me, the one big thing that rivaled Jesus for first place in my life was football. A big part of my dream of playing football was to be the quarterback at Baylor University. As a kid growing up, I loved Baylor, where my dad had played football in the early 1950s. I was a dyed-in-the-wool Baylor Bear cub almost from the womb.

Those of us who grew up loving the Baylor Bears during the '50s and '60s also despised the Texas Longhorns who dominated college football – including us – during the 1960s. When I stepped onto the campus as a freshman, Baylor hadn't beaten Texas in fourteen years, our last win coming when I was only three years old! In 1971, my first year at Baylor, Texas beat us 24-0 – our fifteenth loss to them in a row. My sophomore year the streak stretched to sixteen years:

Texas 17, Baylor 3. In my junior year we played Texas at Memorial Stadium in Austin before 81,000-plus fans and they thumped us 42-6. It was seventeen years and counting since Baylor had beaten Texas.

On November 9, 1974, in my senior year, the Longhorns rolled into Waco ranked seventh in the country. We were having a pretty good year, too, so it was a big conference showdown on the Brazos River that borders our campus. The stadium only held about 48,000, but on that day more than 54,000 pumped-up fans jammed into the place.

On the third play of the game I hit receiver Alcy Jackson with a pass on the left sideline. He broke a tackle and raced 67 yards for a touchdown. The place went crazy! We were ahead 7-0. Everybody was thinking, *Maybe this is the year we finally beat Texas!* Well, the NCAA rules are very clear. Once your team scores, you have to kick the ball to the other team. So we kicked off to Texas, and they marched down the field with ease and tied the game. A few minutes later they scored again to take a 14-7 lead.

We got the ball and worked down the field into Texas territory, then I threw an interception. As I remember, it wasn't my fault; the receiver ran the wrong route. He may claim that I threw to the wrong spot, but it's my book, so we're remembering it my way! Anyway, Texas methodically took the ball down the field and scored another touchdown, widening the lead to 21-7. The Longhorns closed out the first half by kicking a field goal, now leading 24-7.

Well, tons of our fans had seen enough. They had watched Texas beat Baylor seventeen years in a row, and they did not want to watch it happen again. So at halftime they left the stadium by the thousands.

Miracle on the Brazos

Texas received the second half kickoff and our defense stopped them in three plays, forcing them to punt. Our guys blocked the punt and recovered the ball. We drove down to the one-yard line, decided to go for it on fourth down and scored a touchdown, trimming the Texas lead to 24-14. The Baylor defense, which did a spectacular job throughout the entire second half, managed to stop

Texas, and we scored again: Texas 24, Baylor 21. Then Texas put together a great drive deep into our territory. But our free safety put a major hit on the Texas quarterback who fumbled the ball, and we recovered. Our offense charged down the field and I threw what I must admit was an incredible pass for a touchdown, giving us the lead, 28-24. All of a sudden the fans who had left the stadium at halftime, but were listening on the radio, started rushing back into the stadium.

All of a sudden the fans who had left the stadium at halftime, but were listening on the radio, started rushing back into the stadium.

In the fourth quarter, we kicked two field goals, and as the clock wound down we were leading the University of Texas 34-24, having scored twenty-seven unanswered second-half points. I remember being in the huddle with just seconds left in the game. I was thinking, *This is the greatest experience of my life! I have dreamed and worked a lifetime to do what I have just done!* It was hard to believe what was happening to me because things this great didn't happen to me. I had weird thoughts that it was only a dream or that Texas would somehow score an eleven-point touchdown to win the game.

Then the gun sounded and the game was over. Only an athlete knows what it's like to stand on the field, arms raised in total elation, having just won the greatest victory of his life. Fans stormed the field and cheerleaders hugged and kissed everyone. On the field and in the locker room it was just an incredible celebration! I'm convinced it was one of the greatest comebacks in the history of Earth. OK, maybe I'm exaggerating just a bit, but for lifetime Baylor fans that's what it felt like!

Late that Saturday night I was on my way home to the dorm at Baylor when I remembered that the university president had said that if we ever beat Texas, he would leave the scoreboard lights on all night in honor of the victory. So I decided to drive out to the stadium and take a look. I climbed up a stone wall at the stadium opposite the scoreboard and there it was, blazing in the night: Baylor 34, Texas 24. I stood there for a long time soaking up the moment of a lifetime, having just fulfilled a lifelong dream.

Standing on that stadium wall staring at the scoreboard, I felt something down in my heart of hearts, deep in my soul. You know what? I'll bet many people have felt the exact same thing. Having just fulfilled my biggest dream, here's what I felt: *It just wasn't enough!* My great experience didn't satisfy me the way I always thought it would. It didn't fill me up the way I thought it would. I realized that football could be on the list of big things in my life, but football could never satisfy me. Therefore, football didn't have the right to be first on my list, the number one thing in my life.

Here's the big idea I want to share with you: *Whatever you allow to be the number one thing in your life will define who you are, reveal what you value, shape how you live, and determine your success.* The ability to successfully redeem your time on earth boils down to what you choose as the most important thing in your life.

Nothing Beats Number One

Since football wasn't worthy of being my one thing, I realized that Jesus had to be first in my life. Why? Because Jesus Christ is always enough; He always fills and satisfies. How many teens focus all their energy trying to break into the popular crowd at school only to find out when they get there that it doesn't satisfy? Friendships and fun with other kids are great, but these things don't deserve to be number one because they can't fill your life. Only Jesus can do that.

How many men and women spend a lifetime pursuing power, prestige, fame, acclaim, significance and wealth at the cost of losing a marriage or alienating their kids? And when they get everything the world has to offer, they discover they're no longer interested because it doesn't fill the emptiness inside. The only thing that can fill the emptiness in the human heart is knowing Jesus Christ as Lord.

Whatever you elevate to number one in your life has a huge bearing on how you live and get through each day's challenges. Your number one thing will greatly influence your ability to dream because it will shape your life, focus your attention, and ultimately determine your future. In his book *Halftime*, Bob

Buford talks about how important it is that you put the right thing "in your box," meaning what you choose to be number one in life. He writes:

> What's in your box? Is it money? Career? Family? Freedom? Remember, you can only have one thing in the box. Regardless of your position in life, once you have identified what's in your box, you will be able to see the cluster of activities – surrounded by quiet times for spiritual disciplines, reading and reflecting – that put into play your "one thing" and keep you growing.[1]

The one thing you put in your box will make all the difference in your life, so you need the right one thing:

- *One thing* that will determine your perspective on life and life's handicaps, disappointments, hurts and defeats.
- *One thing* that will enable you to enjoy what the Bible calls a state of joy and blessedness.
- *One thing* that will help you find purpose in life and the passion to live that life.
- *One thing* that will settle the issue of why you are alive and who you are living for. Many people have too much to live *with* – stuff, activities, problems – but nothing to live *for*.
- *One thing* that will be the most essential part of you, that will determine the truth about you, who you are, and who you are capable of becoming.

That's a tall order for only *one* thing, but that's what I really need and want in my life. It must be something big enough to handle everything I will face today, tomorrow, next week, next year and forever. It must be something big enough to transform the negatives in my life – such as stuttering – into positives. It must be something that can turn my life around and make sense of it all, to redeem even my mistakes and messes and use them for a good purpose. And it must be big enough to handle our final enemy, which is death. For all these reasons, the one thing in my box is God's Son, Jesus Christ. Jesus is and has *eternal value*. Since He lasts forever and I am in Him, I also have eternal value.

---

1 Bob Buford, *Halftime: Changing Your Game Plan from Success to Significance* (Grand Rapids, MI: Zondervan, 1997), p.53.

Do you know when life really begins? It begins when you put Jesus Christ in your box as your one thing and reorder your life around Him. Significance comes when you give yourself to God. It changes your attitude and how you see everything!

Two Questions

Just knowing that Jesus is number one in everything doesn't mean that He is number one in your life. His preeminence is not an option for the galaxies and black holes and atoms in the universe because Jesus Christ reigns supremely all around us. But Christ's reign *is* an option for the human heart. It's a matter of our choice, our invitation. That's why I want to ask you two questions.

First, is Jesus the one thing in your life? Have you personally accepted Jesus Christ to be your Savior and Lord? Has there been a moment in time when you bowed your heart and said, "Lord, I'm a sinner and I need a Savior"?

I grew up going to church and Sunday school, and I knew all about Jesus. Then one day as a sophomore in high school, I got down on my knees and asked Jesus Christ to come into my life. It's a decision everyone must make for himself or herself. It's an invitation that only you can extend; no one can do it for you. The Lord of the universe takes His rightful place in your heart only when you surrender the throne of your life to Him. You can accept Jesus at any time, even right now. It's as simple as a few sincere words uttered from your heart in prayer, but the implications of that prayer will impact every single day of your life on earth and for all the eons of eternity.

Second question: Where does Jesus rank in the priorities of your life? Remember, He deserves and demands first place. He is Lord above all things in heaven and earth. Is He Lord over all things in your life? Where is He on your list of priorities?

Many years ago a publisher asked a distinguished panel of twenty-eight historians, educators and journalists to rank what they considered to be the 100 most significant events in history. When the results came in, number one on the list was Columbus discovering America. Second was the development of the printing press with moveable type by Johannes Gutenberg. Eleven events tied for third place. A five-way tie for fourth place included the U.S. Constitution taking effect; the use of ether to make surgery painless; the discovery of x-ray; the successful flight of the Wright brothers' plane; and the crucifixion of Jesus Christ. Jesus made the top 100 but was rated no higher than fourth place on the list along with four other events!

My question for you is: Where is Jesus on your list? If there's not much evidence in the way you live that Jesus occupies first place, then it's pretty clear that He is not number one. However, when Jesus occupies His rightful place at the top of your priorities, it will be evident in how you live day by day.

> *...when Jesus occupies His rightful place at the top of your priorities, it will be evident in how you live day by day.*

Somebody may say, "If it's such a big deal that Jesus take first place in our lives, why doesn't He just snap his fingers and make it happen? I mean, He's God, He's all-powerful. He can just say, 'All right, I'm taking charge. End of story.' And we wouldn't have a choice in the matter." I've wondered about that, too. We human beings can do whatever we want to do. We're not forced to accept Jesus Christ. We can say, "Thanks, but no thanks." We can live our entire lifetime without acknowledging that God even exists – and many people do. We can go through life speaking the name of Jesus Christ only as a curse word. Why would He allow such things?

Maybe God lets people say no to Him so that when they say yes, it really means something. If we were forced to say yes without the option of saying no, our yes means little. But if we have the freedom to say, "No, Jesus, I don't want you to be King of my life. I'm going my own way," then choosing to say yes means something. It's kind of like when I popped the "Will you marry me?" question to Sheila many years ago. If she'd been forced to say yes, it wouldn't have meant much. But Sheila had the choice to say yes or no. She could have said something like, "You're a nice guy, Neal, but I love this other guy more than you, so have a great life." But instead, she said yes, and it meant the world to me!

She was saying, "I love *you*. I choose *you*. I want to be with *you* instead of any other man in the world." That's huge!

Maybe this is the reason God allows us to choose to put Him first instead of forcing us to put Him first. When we say yes to God, it also means we are saying no to any and every other "god" out there that could be wrongly elevated to the place that only God deserves. In so many words we are saying, "Lord, I reject everything in the universe I could devote my life to and serve, and I choose to acknowledge and serve You alone. I want You to occupy first place in my life today, tomorrow and forever."

So what's in your box? If it's anything other than Jesus Christ, you are in danger of missing God's great plans for you. Now is the time to invite Jesus into your life and make Him your number one thing today and forever!

How do you do this? By praying a simple prayer something like this: *Dear Lord, I know that I am a sinner and in need of a Savior. I confess my sin and claim your forgiveness. I believe in You – now I trust You and invite You into my heart to take control of my life and make me the person You want me to be. Thank you for saving me. In Jesus' name, Amen.* If you prayed this prayer sincerely, you are a new Christian. Now share your decision with someone, find a church and begin growing as a believer.

Now we're ready to move on to the second critical area for experiencing everything God has planned for you. It's all about your big dreams and His plans for your future!

II

REACH FOR THE STARS
How to View and Value Your Dreams
and Destiny

*Delight yourself also in the Lord
and He shall give you the desires of your heart.*
P S A L M   3 7 : 4

*Always remember, you have within you the strength, the patience
and the passion to reach for the stars to change the world.*
H A R R I E T   T U B M A N

4

Everything Starts with a Dream

Every great accomplishment in history began with a dream. Every best-selling book, every time-saving invention, every awe-inspiring work of art, every life-saving medical breakthrough and every world record in sports was first a dream deep in someone's heart. Great things happen when people dream what might be and then believe and work hard to make that dream a reality.

Dreaming great dreams is a huge part of achieving great things in life. I'm talking about big dreams, *great* dreams! Don't waste the days and years of your life pursuing just anything. Don't settle for the ordinary. Dream big. Dream *huge.* T.E. Lawrence, the British soldier and adventurer made famous in the film *Lawrence of Arabia*, said, "Dreamers...are dangerous men, for they may act on their dreams with open eyes, to make them possible."

Where did Mozart's magnificent symphonies come from? They began with a dream in the music-filled heart and mind of a creative genius. What about the entertainment empire of the late Jim Henson, the creator of the Muppets? All those lovable characters – Kermit, Oscar the Grouch, Miss Piggy, Cookie Monster – were inside Henson's brain, and he would not let go of his Muppet dream until they came to life on Sesame Street.

Think of anyone who has made a significant contribution to history –

people such as Michelangelo, Abraham Lincoln, Susan B. Anthony, George Washington Carver, Thomas Edison, Albert Einstein, Madam Curie, Martin Luther King Jr. – the list is endless. All the great and helpful things these people gave to the world began with the tiny spark of a dream. Walt Disney spoke for thousands and thousands of great achievers when he said, "All our dreams can come true, if we have the courage to pursue them."

You're Never Too Young or Too Old to Dream

I love little kids because they dream big dreams. Ask a bunch of fourth graders what they want to be when they grow up and you'll get big answers: an astronaut; President of the United States; a doctor who will find a cure for cancer; a lawyer; a millionaire; a movie star. Little kids are not bothered by what others think. They don't care if somebody laughs at them. They just have big dreams – things they want to do when they grow up – and they are innocent enough to believe they can achieve them.

All of us had huge dreams as kids. Do you remember yours? Maybe you're embarrassed to tell anyone about them. But if you had to take a dose of truth serum and reveal your childhood dreams, I bet they would be as big and glorious as the ones listed above.

You already know what my big dream was as a kid – playing professional football on Sundays and throwing passes in super slow motion with great jamming, rocking music in the background. There's a story behind this dream, of course. When I was a kid, we couldn't get any "live" football games on the networks or cable channels like ESPN. All we had was one football show every week produced by NFL Films, and I lived for that show! They would film these great quarterbacks in action – I'm talking about legends like Joe Namath, Johnny Unitas and Bart Starr – throwing passes in super slow motion. They would show the ball up close, spiraling perfectly through the air, with this great jamming, rocking music in the background. I mean, I was glued to that TV! And I thought, *I want to be one of those guys who throws footballs in super slow motion with great jamming, rocking music!*

As I grew older, my big dreams just got bigger. I was going to play football at Baylor University, play in the NFL, be named an All-Pro, get elected to the National Football League Hall of Fame and be remembered as the greatest quarterback that ever lived. Well, I fell a little bit short of some of those goals. But you know what? I don't think I would have gotten as far as I did without those big dreams.

If you're a student in your teens or younger, don't think for a second that you're too young for big dreams and great plans. God used a teenager named Joseph to save his family and the nation of Israel. God used a shepherd boy named David to kill Goliath, the Philistine giant. He used an obedient eight-year-old kid named Josiah to start a great spiritual revival in Israel. And Mary was probably in her teens when an angel told her she would be the mother of Jesus. God also has great things in store for you – both now and in the future. Your dreams are as important to God as the dreams of any adult. And they start here and now, where you are and with what you've got. Start dreaming big now and go for it!

Dreaming is not just for the young. C.S. Lewis wrote, "You are never too old to set another goal or to dream a new dream." The prophet Joel said it this way: "I will pour out My Spirit on all flesh…your old men shall dream dreams" (Joel 2:28). In the Bible, God worked through the dreams of older people just like He did through young people. I mean, where would we be if the great "senior citizens" in the Bible had given up on their dreams and started coasting? At age 600, Noah would have never built the ark that saved his family and the rest of humanity. Abraham and Sarah, each almost 100 years old, would not have become parents to Isaac. Eighty-year-old Moses would have settled for being a shepherd instead of leading Israel out of bondage from Egypt. Old timers Simeon and Anna would have given up waiting long years in the temple for the birth of Jesus.

No matter how old you are, never give up on the dreams God has placed in your heart. Proverbs 13:12 says, "Hope deferred makes the heart sick, but when the desire comes, it is a tree of life." There's no reason why you can't be fulfilling your dreams until the day you die.

Don't Let Go of Your Dreams

You know what a dream does? A dream sticks to your soul; it just won't let you go. A dream demands your best. It makes you start early and stay late. It challenges you and stretches you. You will never go as far as you could go if you don't have a dream. Henry David Thoreau said, "If one advances confidently in the direction of his dreams, and endeavors to live the life which he has imagined, he will meet with a success unexpected in common hours." As you stay locked onto your dreams and apply belief and hard work, those dreams will rise to the surface and materialize as great things in your life.

As you stay locked onto your dreams and apply belief and hard work, those dreams will rise to the surface and materialize as great things in your life.

I love the Olympic Games for many reasons, but the main reason is that the Olympics are what dreams are all about. Every four years athletes from around the world gather in one place to say, "Come watch us accomplish the incredible and the impossible; come watch us fulfill our biggest dreams." It's a thrill to watch victorious athletes during the medal ceremony. The gold medalist mounts the medal platform, flanked by the silver and bronze winners, and stands there proudly as the world's greatest athlete in his or her event. The gold medal is placed around the champion's neck, their national flag is raised, followed by the playing of their national anthem. It's just a great moment seeing the triumph and emotion on these athletes' faces.

Do you know how these world champions got to that great moment? Years earlier they had a dream that would not let them go; and they pursued that dream to the track, to the playing field, to the court, to the ice rink, to the swimming pool, and right on through the thousands of hours of training, drilling, and lifting weights it took to reach world-class level. In those early days nobody knew who they were or how great they would be. All they had was their dream, the belief that they could make it, and the commitment to do everything necessary to reach the top. Then one day they stepped onto the medal platform and proclaimed to the world, "I have accomplished my dream. I made it to the top. This is what can happen when you dream big dreams, believe that you can live that dream, and work hard to realize that dream." Do you know what people think when they see those triumphant athletes on the medal stand? They think, "If he can get through all the obstacles in his life and accomplish something great, so can I. If she can fulfill her dreams, so can I."

Now, I'm not saying that anybody who dreams of becoming an Olympic champion – or an NFL quarterback or a corporate CEO or a prima ballerina and so on – will necessarily realize their dream. The idea is to dream great dreams and to pursue them and live them to the best of your ability. That way, whether you fulfill all your dreams or not, you will accomplish great things you would never have accomplished otherwise.

Seeing others pursue their dreams is contagious. There's a great story from the Olympics that illustrates this point. In 1920, the fastest man in the world was named Charlie Paddock, the Olympic champion in the 100-meter dash. He returned home to America after the Games as a national hero. He went on tour and made speeches all over the country. One day he made a speech at East Tech High School in Cleveland, Ohio. In that speech he said something like, "Who knows, there may be an Olympic champion in this room today. To reach that goal, you've got to have a dream, you've got to believe, you've got to have faith in yourself, and you've got to work hard."

After the speech, Paddock was on the side of the stage answering questions and signing autographs. A young kid stepped up and said, "Mr. Paddock, I want to be just like you." Paddock stopped and looked at the kid. "You *can* be like me," he said, "if you dream, if you have faith. If you work hard, you can be a champion." That kid from East Tech High School in Cleveland, Ohio, was on the U.S. track team in the 1936 Olympics in Berlin, Germany. He won four gold medals, one of them in the 100-meter dash. He was the fastest man in the world, just like his idol Charlie Paddock. That young man's name was Jesse Owens.

Owens came home to America after the Games as a national hero. During a parade in Cleveland, a bunch of kids rushed around his convertible, made them stop the car, and Jesse Owens signed autographs and answered questions from his young fans. One of the kids said, "Mr. Owens, I want to be an Olympic champion just like you." Jesse looked up at the kid and said, "Son, you can be a champion if you dream, if you have faith, and if you believe you can do it." This kid was so skinny that everybody called him "Bones." Well, Bones ran all the way home and told his grandmother, "I'm going to be an Olympic champion just like Jesse Owens." In the 1948 Olympic Games, the man who won the gold medal in the 100-meter dash, the fastest man in the world, was named Harrison "Bones" Dillard.

Here's a key idea: *No matter how young you are or how old you are, if you can dream great dreams, you can accomplish great things.* As someone has said, "No dreamer is ever too small; no dream is ever too big." Yes, it will take time. Yes, it may be a tough, uphill climb. Yes, fulfilling your dream will take faith and hard work. Jesse Owens once said, "Turning your dreams into reality takes an awful lot of determination, dedication, self-discipline and effort." But if dreams, belief and hard work can turn people like Walt Disney, Michelangelo, Charlie Paddock, Jesse Owens and "Bones" Dillard into champions in their fields, they can do the same for you.

Impossible Dreams Are Possible

As a junior high kid with stars in my eyes, a big dream in my heart, and a severe stuttering problem, there was one question that *never* crossed my mind: "What chance do I really have of becoming the greatest quarterback ever, let alone playing football at Baylor and in the NFL?" I wasn't blind to my speech problem – far from it. But it never occurred to me that my stuttering could keep me from becoming the next Bart Starr or Johnny Unitas. Others may have looked at me and said, "Impossible. No way will that kid make it to major college football and the NFL." But I was blinded to the impossibilities by the light of my own dream, and I was going to do whatever it took to fulfill that dream.

Here's one of the ways I kept my dream alive as a kid. Before every game I played in junior high and senior high, I would go through the same ritual.

I'd come home from school on game day afternoon, get something to eat, and then go into my parents' bedroom. They had a hi-fi set in there, one of those big pieces of furniture with a record player and huge speakers in it. I would pull out an LP record by Andy Williams. Now if you don't know what a hi-fi or an LP is or who Andy Williams is, don't sweat it. Ask your parents or grandparents. They'll know. Anyway, Andy Williams could really sing. I'd put his record on the turntable and drop the needle on a particular song. Then I'd lie on the bed, stare up the ceiling and listen. When the song was finished, I'd play it again and again and again.

> *I was blinded to the impossibilities by the light of my own dream, and I was going to do whatever it took to fulfill that dream.*

The song I always listened to was "The Impossible Dream" from the Broadway musical *The Man from La Mancha*. This song is a classic. It's all about righting the unrightable wrong, beating the unbeatable foe, striving with your last ounce of courage…to reach the unreachable star! It's an incredible song that fired me up! By the time I got to the football field after listening to Andy Williams sing that song a few times, I was ready to play ball! It didn't matter how big the other team was or how good they were. I played like my teammates and I were unbeatable. Did we win every game? No, far from it. But thanks in part to the inspiration I got from that song to be both a dreamer and a doer, I played every game like I believed we could win it!

It's awesome to have a big dream for your life and to pursue, accomplish and live that dream. While football was that dream for me, you have your own story of reaching some dreams. Maybe you're a student athlete who is finding success in your sport because of your dreams and hard work. Or maybe you always hoped to adopt a child or two and now a couple of these kids call you "Mom" or "Dad." Maybe you dreamed of retiring early in order to do volunteer work serving the needy, and now you're living that dream.

As awesome as those dreams are, there is something even more awesome. It's allowing God to do a supernatural work *in* you that accomplishes supernatural actions *through* you. Dreaming great dreams is not only about discovering what you can achieve and accomplish with your God-given abilities, but also about discovering what the God who gave you those abilities can do in and through you. There are no greater dreams than the dreams God created for you and called you to fulfill.

Now I'm not saying that earthly dreams and goals such as playing football, succeeding in business or being recognized as "Teacher of the Year" are unimportant; but if your dreams are attached only to this world, you haven't experienced the greater thrill of seeing what God can accomplish supernaturally through you. God has something greater for you to do than winning a championship, having a three-car garage with three shiny cars, marrying the right person or having perfect kids – and there's nothing wrong with any of these. God has a supernatural plan for your life, and He wants to use you to accomplish that plan in a powerful way.

An incredible story in the next chapter about a man named Edward illustrates what can happen when someone taps into God's plans and determines to live them out.

5

Get Out of the Boat

Edward was real nervous when he walked up to the door of the shoe store. He had to go into the store because God had *told* him to. He put his hand on the doorknob but chickened out at the last second. He turned away and paced the sidewalk, trying to pump up his courage. Edward wanted to do what God asked him to do, but the idea of confronting a clerk he barely knew and talking to him about Jesus scared him spitless.

He passed the door a couple more times before he sucked it up and stepped inside. Edward hoped that the clerk was off today or had gone home early. But no such luck. There he was in the rear of the store. *No turning back now*, Edward thought. Waiting for the right opportunity, he followed the clerk into the stockroom. Asking for a moment of the clerk's time, Edward told him about Christ's love and offer of salvation. To Edward's surprise and relief, the young clerk listened attentively and accepted Christ as his Savior on the spot!

That happened in 1858, and that young shoe clerk named Dwight L. Moody went on to become one of the greatest evangelists the world has ever known. And it all started with an ordinary guy named Edward Kimball who stepped out with fear and faith to tell a shoe salesman that God loved him. But the story doesn't end with D.L. Moody. Moody's preaching influenced a string of people, including a man named Billy Sunday who accepted Christ as Savior. Sunday also became a powerful evangelist in the early twentieth century. His influence filtered down to the city of Charlotte, North Carolina, where a young farm boy gave his life to Christ. That boy's name was Billy Graham.

Think about it. Dwight Moody, Billy Sunday and Billy Graham are among the most influential evangelists of all time. What if Edward Kimball had walked away from that shoe store without talking to Moody? Well, we don't have to wonder about it because Kimball stepped up and did what God told him to do in spite of his fear, and great things happened.

Edward Kimball discovered something about trusting God that every one of us desperately needs to discover. Experiencing God's plan is not about finding out what *you* can do – it's about finding out what *God* can do *through* you. It's not about how strong you are – it's about how strong God is as He works through you. It's not about how big your muscles are – it's about how big God's muscles are and what His power can accomplish through you.

Here's what I want you to see: *You may be able to accomplish a lot in your own strength and through your own drive and persistence, but only God can accomplish in you and through you the supernatural plan He has for your life.* This is life on a completely different level. This is where you rise above the ordinary to experience the extraordinary. In short, this is where you encounter miracles in your life.

Falter in Fear or Follow in Faith?

What kind of miracles are we talking about here? Well, we're talking about miracles like the ones you find in the New Testament. I'm thinking about one that's familiar to most people. It's where Jesus walks on water. He had just finished feeding 5,000 people using only a boy's small lunch, which is a pretty huge miracle in itself. Matthew 14 tells us what happened next.

> *Immediately, Jesus made His disciples get into the boat and go before Him to the other side, while He sent the multitudes away. And when He had sent the multitudes away, He went up on the*

mountain by Himself to pray. Now when evening came, He was alone there. But the boat was now in the middle of the sea, tossed by the waves, for the wind was contrary. Now in the fourth watch of the night, Jesus went to them, walking on the sea. (Matthew 14: 22-25)

Now just to remind you, walking on top of the water is a miracle. This is huge – totally a God thing. No other human being in the history of the world has ever done it. It had never happened before, so it's no wonder the disciples reacted the way they did. Verse 26 says, "When the disciples saw Him walking on the sea, they were troubled, saying, 'It is a ghost!' And they cried out for fear." The disciples thought it had to be a ghost because no man could walk on water – no way!

Verse 27 says, "But immediately Jesus spoke to them, saying, 'Be of good cheer! It is I; do not be afraid.'" What a great truth! Jesus is saying, "Your Savior and Master is here, so you don't have to be afraid." How encouraging is that? Whatever storm you're facing today, you are not alone. Jesus is right there with you.

Then Peter speaks up. "Lord, if it is You, command me to come to You on the water" (v.28). Now that's amazing. Peter has just seen Jesus walk on the water, something nobody in the history of the world has ever done before, a total miracle. And Peter's response is, "Lord, let me do it, too! I want to come out to you walking on the water." Do you realize what he's asking for? He's asking to do the impossible. He's asking for the supernatural to happen. He's asking to be part of a miracle.

Then another amazing thing happens. In verse 29, Jesus said, "Come." He could have said, "Stay. You don't know what you're asking for, big guy. This is God stuff out here. This is not for ordinary humans. You stay put." But no, Peter asked for the impossible and Jesus said one word, "Come." I think the point Jesus was making went something like this: "If you've got the faith to get out of that boat and step out on the water, then come on! You're not going to see what *you* can do – you're going to see what *I* can do."

Watch what happens next. "And when Peter had come down out of the boat, he walked on the water to go to Jesus" (v.29). A couple of quick questions: First, if it's a miracle when Jesus walks on the water, what do you call it when Peter walks on the water? No-brainer, it's a miracle, too! Second, when did Peter's miracle begin? It began when he got out of the boat.

Here's the big challenge: *You will never rise above your limitations and handicaps to experience the dreams God has for you until you get out of the boat.* Like Peter, you have to step out of your comfort zone, out of what you know you can do, in order for Jesus to do something in you that is beyond your ability and understanding. If you settle for a dream you can achieve in your own strength and intelligence, you will never experience what God can make of you and accomplish through you. If you allow your weaknesses and defeats to limit what you attempt in this life, you will miss the thrill of seeing God turn them into strengths and victories.

Miracles Happen When You Get Out of the Boat

A miracle never would have happened if Peter had stayed in the boat. But for some reason, Peter was courageous enough to step out of the comfort zone of a boat – the only disciple to do it. Do you think Peter was afraid of getting out of the boat and taking that first step? Well, think about it. Peter asked to go where no man except Jesus had ever gone. If he didn't feel some amount of fear and doubt, he wouldn't be human. Of course he was afraid. Yet because he climbed out of the boat, a supernatural event happened.

❖

...you must first put yourself in miracle territory by stepping out of the comfort zone of security into the miracle zone of faith.

❖

Back in 1858, a miracle never would have happened if Edward Kimball had stayed on the sidewalk outside that shoe store. Was he afraid? Was he unsure of himself? Did he have doubts that anything good would happen? Of course, who wouldn't? But he "got out of the boat." And when he stepped out of his comfort and security zone and walked through the doorway, Edward Kimball became a candidate for the miracle God was ready to perform.

When you think of the dreams you want to pursue and the tasks God is calling you to do, do you feel afraid? If so, that's good. Fear in the face of a challenge proves a couple of things. First, it proves you're human, because everybody experiences a certain amount of fear when they face new and challenging experiences. Second, your anxiety means that you're probably reaching beyond what you can accomplish in your own strength. Just like Peter, you're in a spot where God can do big things. But for miracles to happen, you must first put yourself in miracle territory by stepping out of the comfort zone of security into the miracle zone of faith.

Called to Walk on Water

When I was a senior in high school, God called me to get out of the boat and walk on water. Well, not literally, but what He asked me to do was just as scary. He called me to become a preacher. I would sit in church on Sundays and listen to our pastor preach and challenge people to accept Christ and serve Him. Down deep inside I sensed God saying, "Neal, I want you to speak for me, too."

Big problem. As a senior in high school I couldn't even talk without stuttering severely. I mean, I couldn't talk on the phone. I couldn't say a simple "Hi" to people. I couldn't carry on a normal conversation. I especially couldn't speak in front of a group. I couldn't even say a silent prayer without stuttering! Yet I had this strong feeling in my gut that God was calling me to be a preacher, something that involves speaking, of course – a *lot* of speaking. No way was I ready to sign on for that. But God has a way of getting His point across. Let me share a couple of examples.

As a senior in high school, I was part of a small youth choir from our church. One thing most stutterers can do without stuttering is sing, so being in the choir was no problem for me. One Sunday, however, when we were presenting a concert at another church, Larry our director said to us in front of the congregation, "Students, I want each of you to introduce yourselves. Say your name and where you go to school."

Well, the moment he said that I'm thinking, "Oh no, I'm going to make a fool of myself! I'm going to stutter and get stuck and not be able to say anything!" The other kids ahead of me were introducing themselves, and I'm getting more terrified by the minute. Finally, my turn comes. All I need to say is, "I'm Neal Jeffrey, and I'm a senior at Shawnee Mission South High School." But when I opened my mouth, nothing came out. I was just totally stuck. And, of course, when a stutterer gets in a pressure situation like that, he panics. Everything freezes up and nothing comes out.

So there I am with my mouth hanging open and every eye in the place looking at me. I can feel the embarrassment of my friends and see the horrified looks on the faces of the audience. I know what they're thinking: *Man, what's wrong with that kid? His mouth is open, but nothing is happening.* After what seemed like forever, Larry interrupted me. Technically, I guess he didn't interrupt me because I hadn't said anything. But he stepped into the awkward situation and said, "That's Neal Jeffrey, a senior at Shawnee Mission South High School." It was one of the most humiliating experiences of my life. I could feel my face turning bright red. I could sense all my friends feeling sorry for me. I wanted to run out of that church and just keep running. And on top of it all I'm thinking, *God wants me to be a preacher? There's no way!*

During my freshman year at Baylor I was involved in a large, active Fellowship of Christian Athletes group on campus. I was among several Baylor athletes who attended a national Weekend of Champions Conference at Texas Tech University in Lubbock. On Friday night when we arrived at the hotel where all the athletes were staying, there was this big board posted in the lobby. Down the left side of the board were the names of all the athletes. Next to each name was printed where that athlete would be sharing his or her testimony on Sunday. FCA had arranged for every church in Lubbock to have a guest Christian athlete or coach sharing a testimony.

When I saw my name on the big board, I freaked out! Somebody had made a big mistake. For obvious reasons, I had not volunteered to give my testimony anywhere on Sunday. But next to my name on the big board was the name of a church where I was scheduled to speak on Sunday. Well, I had to get out of that assignment. I found my FCA sponsor Friday night and asked him to do something, but he was no help. All day Saturday I stressed about that assignment. I just knew it would be another humiliating disaster. I thought about possible excuses for getting out of it – that I was sick or injured, that a relative had died suddenly back home, anything! If the Baylor campus in Waco hadn't been six hours from Lubbock, I would have started walking. No way did I want to embarrass myself in front of another group.

But on Sunday morning, there I was at the church waiting to be introduced. The crystal clear, terrifying truth dawned on me: *There is no way out. I have to do this. I have to stand up in front of that congregation of strangers and make a fool of myself. I will stutter through the whole thing and it will be another disaster.* As I was being introduced, I remember saying to God, *You've got to do something, like blow up the sound system so I don't have to speak. Please don't let me be humiliated again.*

The next thing I knew I was standing behind the pulpit with everybody looking at me. All I could do was put my eyes on Jesus and step out of the boat. I took a deep breath, opened my mouth, and began speaking. And for the first time in my life, I spoke five to seven minutes straight without one stutter! I mean, the words just rolled out of me. I didn't even feel any tension in my chest. Usually my neck and chest are sore because of the physical stress of trying to

And for the first time in my life, I spoke five to seven minutes straight without one stutter!

speak. I remember thinking as I was speaking, *Who is this?* I had never before experienced such a free flow of words. It was incredible!

When I finished my talk and sat down, I was in awe. You know what I discovered that day? Not how great Neal Jeffrey is, because I knew I couldn't do what I had just done. I discovered firsthand how great God is, how big God is, how powerful God is, and that God can do anything! He is not limited to my puny excuses for what I can and cannot do. He is a God who can do "exceedingly abundantly above all that we ask or think, according to the power that works in us" (Ephesians 3:20).

Later that year I was asked to speak at the National Fellowship of Christian Athletes' Summer Conference on the campus of Colorado State University in Fort Collins. I was to give my testimony in the same meeting that my coach at Baylor was to be the keynote speaker. I assumed that God would show up again, and I would be able to speak fluently just as I did at that church in Lubbock.

But when I stood up to share my testimony, hardly anything I said came out right. I stuttered so much I wasn't sure anything I said was understandable. I remember feeling so frustrated, so helpless, so embarrassed, but I kept going through the whole message. My topic was the same as it had been in Lubbock. I told the story from the New Testament about Jesus feeding 5,000 people using a little boy's lunch of five loaves of bread and two fish. The point of my talk was to give whatever you have to Jesus, and He will use it for His glory and to accomplish His purposes.

Well, I finished my talk and walked off the stage thinking I had just blown it, that nothing good had been accomplished. But to my shock, over 800 high school and college athletes from across America gave me a standing ovation. Also, several of my friends from Baylor made commitments to Jesus Christ after the service.

Here is the point: *God used me both times – when He allowed me to speak very well, and when He allowed me to stutter very well.* Both times His work was accomplished. God showed me through these completely different experiences that all He needs is a willing vessel to work through. Whether I stutter or not, He can use it all! Do you know how I made these discoveries? By getting out of the boat! When I stepped up and opened my mouth, I was out of my comfort zone and into the faith zone. I was on the open sea where only Jesus could get me through. If I had weaseled out of those speaking assignments, I would have totally missed the awesome thing God was preparing me for.

Miracles happen when we step by faith beyond what we can do and trust God to do what only He can do. I have been a pastor, conference speaker, and corporate motivational speaker for almost thirty years. There is no way I get to this point in my life on my own. I'm a stutterer. Listen to me: stutterers don't succeed as public speakers. It's impossible. And yet here I am. There's only one way to explain it: God's grace and power.

Get Out of the Boat Daily

I don't want you to think that what God has done in my life was a one-time miracle. Every day I get out of bed I have to get out of the boat again and trust God for His miracles. That day in Lubbock when the words rolled out of me unhindered, well, that day has never happened again. I still stutter. The miracle is that as I step out and speak, God seems to step in and work.

That day in Lubbock when the words rolled out of me unhindered, well, that day has never happened again. I still stutter.

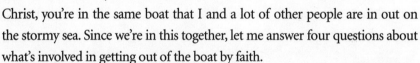

Every day of my life I am faced with opportunities to get out of the boat and trust God. And if you are a follower of Christ, you're in the same boat that I and a lot of other people are in out on the stormy sea. Since we're in this together, let me answer four questions about what's involved in getting out of the boat by faith.

1. How do I prepare to get out of the boat? You ask God to call you out. That's what Peter did. Your daily prayer could be something like, "Lord, I welcome your invitation for me to step out of my comfort zone and trust you." Yes, it's a scary prayer because God may ask you to do something that seems impossible to you. But it is also an exciting prayer because God is always ready to do the impossible.

2. How do I know when God wants me to get out of the boat? You listen for His call. Jesus said to Peter, "come," and Jesus will say "come" to you in many different ways if you're listening for it. He says "come" through his Word. For example, you're reading the Bible or listening to the sermon in church and something jumps out at you. You feel an impression to do something that seems way too big for you. He also says "come" through his Spirit inside you. Like Edward Kimball, you may hear God whispering in your soul or giving you an impression to do something special. God also says "come" through the wisdom and counsel of other believers, and even through circumstances. Like my experience as a freshman in Lubbock, God lets you get into situations where there's no one you can trust but Him.

3. How do I get out of the boat in the middle of a "storm"? You keep your eyes on the One who called you out, not on yourself or your circumstances. When Peter got out of the boat and started walking on the water, he did fine as long as he focused on Jesus. It was only when he "saw that the wind was boisterous" (v.30) that he panicked, took his eyes off Jesus and began to sink. We get that sinking feeling, too, if we're distracted by the impossible situations God calls us into. That's why we must keep our eyes on Him, because no situation is impossible for Him.

4. What happens if I fail or if things don't work out right? You reach out to Jesus in faith, knowing that He will rescue you. Matthew 14:31 says that Peter didn't save himself – Jesus reached out His hand to Peter. The beautiful principle is: When God calls you to do something and you respond obediently in faith, He is ultimately responsible for the results. Your part is to step out when He says "come," keep your eyes fixed on Him, and trust Him to take care of the rest.

Can you imagine what miraculous things God wants to do through you as you pursue your dreams and His plans for your life? All you have to do to find out is take that step of faith and keep your eyes on Him, and in no time you'll be "walking on water."

6

Learning to Walk on Water

One chilly November day, a mother and her two young sons huddled together against a biting wind. They watched as two men shoveled dirt into an open grave. The woman wept and the boys fought back tears. At the bottom of the grave was the tiny coffin of a two-year-old girl – the woman's daughter and the boys' little sister. Next to the open grave was another grave that belonged to the woman's husband who had died suddenly the previous year.

Mary Ann Bickerdyke felt empty as she watched her little girl's coffin lowered into the ground that day. Why had God taken these two precious people from her? What good could He possibly bring out of these tragedies? She longed to do something significant for God, but it seemed that He had turned His back on her. What could a plain woman from Galesburg, Illinois – the widowed mother of two small boys – possibly accomplish for God?

A few months after the funeral, the Civil War broke out and thousands of Illinois men marched south to confront the secessionists. One Sunday, the pastor of Mary Ann's church read a letter from a local doctor serving in the army camp in southern Illinois. Many of the soldiers were very sick before they had even seen battle. The doctor was writing to ask the church to send someone with food, medicine and clean blankets for "our boys." Church leaders knew exactly who to send. They asked Mary Ann to take the supplies to the camp and assess the need. But she felt inadequate and fearful. It was dangerous for a woman to travel alone. And who would take care of her sons while she was gone? Yet something stirred within her. Was this a call from God? Was she willing to take a step of faith into the unknown and trust Him?

Like Peter climbing out of the boat, this widow stepped out in faith despite her fear and hesitation and agreed to do the job. And as the old saying goes, the rest is history. Mary Ann Bickerdyke became a Civil War heroine who influenced thousands of lives for decades to come. And it all started when she said yes to something she didn't think she could do.

Three God-things happen when you get out of the boat in response to His invitation. As these things happen, you will find that all the stuff standing between you and your dreams shrinks from mountains to molehills.

Experience a Miracle

The first thing that happens when you get out of the boat is that you may experience a miracle. A miracle is something that can be explained only in terms of supernatural power at work. A miracle happens where human or natural power ends and God's power takes over. Peter's step of faith put him out on the water in a raging storm where God had to come through or he would sink like an anchor. When he stepped out of the boat, the situation was way over his head; but because God came through, the water stayed under his feet and he walked on it! Peter trusted Jesus and walked into a miracle.

When you step outside the comfort zone of your own ability and experience, you put yourself in a situation where God has to come through for you. And that's just where God wants you! Hebrews 11:6 says, "Without faith it is impossible to please Him." If you can handle every situation on your own, you don't need God. You're not walking by faith, and you'll never experience a miracle. What's worse, unless you walk by faith, you'll never be able to get past the defeats and disappointments that have kept you from living out God's plan and purpose for you.

In June of 1861, the forty-three-year-old widow named Mary Ann Bickerdyke left her sons in the care of friends and boarded a train with crates of supplies. She expected to be gone for a week or less, yet that first step of faith launched her on a mission that would occupy the rest of her life, a mission that was so far beyond her comprehension that it seemed impossible. When Mary Ann arrived at the Army camp, she was shocked at how filthy the army hospitals were. Soldiers were dying from disease, malnutrition and neglect – and the army was doing nothing about it! It was wrong and Mary Ann could not return home without doing what she could to make things right. Instead of staying for a few days, she stayed for several months cleaning up hospitals, bathing and feeding sick soldiers, and training other volunteers as nurses and orderlies. Mary Ann's church in Galesburg sent supplies by train and made sure her two sons were cared for.

When the Union troops under General Grant went into battle, Mary Ann Bickerdyke and her team of volunteers went with them to make sure the wounded and sick were properly cared for. The army didn't ask her to do it. In fact, many of the officers and surgeons didn't want her there and resisted her help, which was saving lives and boosting morale. Almost everything about her task was exhausting, unpleasant and beyond her natural abilities. But she continued to work in God's power and earned the respect and admiration of General Grant and General Sherman.

I believe the biggest thing that prevents most of us from experiencing God's miraculous power is our desire for security. We don't like taking chances or putting ourselves in situations we're not sure we can handle. We back away from things that might be unpleasant or embarrassing for us. We steer clear of anything that might demand from us more than we are willing to give. Instead, we seek territory that is safe, comfortable, predictable and manageable.

In my early years as an assistant pastor, our church had a ministry called Evangelism Explosion. In EE, church members were trained to share their faith with others one-on-one. Each participant got a name and address on a card, drove to the home with two other EE trainers, and sat down with people to share the gospel face to face.

I used to dread Wednesday nights because it was EE night. For a stutterer, the scariest thing in life is knocking on the door of a total stranger, because you have to embarrass yourself all over again in front of someone new! But as assistant pastor I was expected to participate. So when Wednesday night rolled around, I got this sick feeling in my stomach. I'd start thinking up excuses why I couldn't participate. Every Wednesday night I wished I was home watching a game on ESPN instead of knocking on the doors of strangers.

> *For a stutterer, the scariest thing in life is knocking on the door of a total stranger, because you have to embarrass yourself all over again in front of someone new!*

But you know what I discovered? Miracles never happened when I sat home watching a ballgame. But they did happen when I was terrified out of my socks and still got out of the boat, knocked on doors and told people about the gift of eternal life. Today, miracles happen in *me* when I trust God to use me – stuttering and all – and miracles happen in *others* I talk to when they accept Christ and discover a new and better way of life.

Some people I talk to doubt that they can experience miracles or be used by God in miraculous ways. They say things like, "My faith isn't that strong" or "I'm not a very mature Christian" or "I'm nobody special." Nowhere in the Bible does it say that you have to do everything perfectly in order to experience God's power and miracles in and through your life. Peter and the other disciples weren't perfect. Edward Kimball and Dwight Moody and Mary Ann Bickerdyke weren't perfect. And I know for sure how weak and imperfect I am. Yet when people step out in faith, God uses them in awesome ways.

Experiencing God's power doesn't depend on how big or mature or special or strong or experienced you are. The issue is your faith in God expressed by your willingness to step out and let God use you. Miracles happen when we trade in the status quo for a lifestyle of higher, swifter, stronger – no matter what it may cost us.

Experience the Touch of Jesus

The second thing that happens when you get out of the boat is that you experience the touch of Jesus. The story in Matthew continues:

> But when [Peter] saw that the wind was boisterous, he was afraid; and beginning to sink he cried out, saying, "Lord save me!" And immediately Jesus stretched out His hand and caught him, and said to him, "O you of little faith, why did you doubt?" And when they got into the boat the wind ceased. (Matthew 14:30-32)

Peter wasn't alone out there on the water; Jesus was with him all the time. When Peter took his eyes off Jesus and began to sink, Jesus stretched out His hand and saved him from drowning. Even though Peter was outside his comfort zone and beyond the border of security and safety, he was never beyond the reach of the Master's touch.

If you have been touched by Jesus Christ, you know you're not the same person you once were. In fact, if you've been touched by Jesus, the people around you know you're not the same – your parents, your spouse, your children, your coworkers, your friends, your neighbors. There is a big difference in your life. You're no longer content to stay in the boat when you can be walking on the water with Jesus. The safety and security of the status quo isn't for you. You live for your dreams and for fulfilling God's plans at any cost. You live by faith; you live on the edge because you know Jesus is right there with you no matter what the outcome may be.

When Mary Ann Bickerdyke left the security of her home to serve God during the Civil War, she ended up living on the edge for four years. She worked in a war zone among soldiers who were sick and dying. She constantly battled opposition from male officers and doctors who resented her presence and blocked her efforts. It was an uphill battle for her all the way. But she would not be stopped because she had experienced the power and touch of Jesus. Once during the height of a battle, an arrogant army surgeon demanded to know who gave her the authority to care for the wounded. Mary replied, "I have been commissioned by the Lord God Almighty. Do you outrank Him?"

The touch of Jesus makes all the difference when you get out of the boat. No matter what God calls you to do, there will be dangers, storms, failures and opposition from others. But when you're in the strong arms of Jesus, you can get through anything, and great things can happen. When you stepped out of the boat and trusted Christ for your salvation, God gave you a brand new life. He reached down and picked you up by His grace even though you didn't deserve it. Talk about a miracle! That was the greatest miracle He could perform in your life, but it was only the first of many He wants you to experience as you follow Him.

How long has it been since you've experienced the touch of the Master's hand by stepping out in response to God's call on your life? He not only wants to save you, He wants to accomplish incredible things through you every day that you live. There is nothing as sweet as discovering and accomplishing His plans and purposes for you through His touch on your life.

Experience Worship

The third thing that happens when you get out of the boat in response to God's call is that you experience worship. After Jesus rescued Peter and calmed the storm, the story ends with this: "Then those who were in the boat came and worshiped Him, saying, 'Truly You are the Son of God'" (Matt. 14:33). The result of the miracle experienced by Peter and the other disciples was that everybody worshiped Jesus as the Son of God.

Worship is the "whoa factor" that comes along with experiencing miracles by getting out of the boat to trust Jesus. In fact, the story could have been told like this.

> All the disciples are in the boat during a storm when they suddenly see Jesus walking on the water, and they all go "Whoa-a-a!" Then the eleven hear their friend Peter ask Jesus if he can walk on the water, and they go "Whoa-a-a!" Then they watch their friend get out of the boat and actually walk

on the water, and they go "Whoa-a-a!" Then they see their friend take his eyes off Jesus and begin to sink. He's going to drown, he's going to die! But Jesus reaches down and says "Whoa-a-a!" and picks him up. And they all go "Whoa-a-a!" Then Jesus gets into the boat, and they all realize that the wind and rain have stopped and the storm is over. They look at Jesus and go, "Whoa-a-a! You are the Son of God!"

All twelve disciples in the boat worshiped Jesus because of what they had just experienced. But you know what? I'll bet you anything that one guy worshiped at a depth the others could not comprehend. You see, eleven of those guys *watched* a miracle; Peter *experienced* a miracle! Eleven guys watched Jesus reach out to Peter and save him. His life was saved by Jesus' touch – a touch that changed him forever.

I have also experienced the "whoa factor" of God's call and miraculous power in my life. I've been super-blessed. But the greatest thrill of my life is that right now I know I'm where God wants me to be and I'm doing what He wants me to do. There's no way I get to do what I'm doing except by the grace and goodness of an incredible God. For some reason He reached out to me and said, "Son, I know you can't do it on your own, but I'm going to do something with you that will blow your mind." Ever since I got out of the boat, it blows my mind to see how God works. *Whoa-a-a!*

For example, I teach a men's Bible study every Friday morning in our church, challenging guys to be the man God wants them to be. How awesome it is when one of our Bible study guys comes up to me and shares how God has used me to make a difference in his life. *Whoa-a-a!* And

I'm telling you, there is no reward in this world as precious as hearing that God has used you to make a difference in someone's life.

sometimes the wife of one of these guys – a woman I don't even know – stops me at church to say with tears in her eyes, "Neal, I just want to thank you. I've seen an incredible change in my husband's life since he's been in the Friday morning Bible study. He is not the same man." That's a big *whoa-a-a!*

I'm telling you, there is no reward in this world as precious as hearing that God has used you to make a difference in someone's life. There is no amount of money in the world that compares to discovering that God is working out His plan through you. That's the blessing of knowing Jesus and following Him in every area of your life and discovering what He can do with you for His glory.

One of the most important things that God wants to do through you is to impact those around you because, whether you realize it or not, you are being watched.

7

You're Being Watched

I've read that an estimated three to four billion people watch the track and field events for the Olympic Games. Imagine being an athlete warming up for your event on the track in the Olympic stadium. You glance over and see a TV camera zooming in on you. Billions of people around the world are ready to watch you compete. What would you be thinking?

Well, two things would be on my mind. First, I'm thinking that I'm going to give this race my ultimate best. All my training, all my experience, everything I've learned – I'm leaving it all on the track. I'm not holding anything back in a race that half the world is going to watch me run. The second thing I'm thinking is that I am not going to pick my nose or do anything stupid or embarrassing in front of a worldwide audience!

Now, it's not likely that you or I will ever do anything that three or four billion people will watch us do, but we are being watched by some very important people; and what these people see as they watch us is making a huge impact on their lives. Here's what I want to emphasize: *When you get out of the boat to live your dream and pursue God's plan for you, make sure you give it everything you've got because your example will deeply impact the people who are watching you.*

Who is watching you? I'm talking about your family members: parents, brothers and sisters, spouse, kids, grandkids and so on. I'm talking about your friends: old and new, near and far, at work, at school, in your neighborhood, in your church. I'm talking about the coworkers or classmates who know you well because you spend so much time together. What you say and do and how you respond to your many opportunities and difficulties is being noticed by those who are closest and dearest to you.

What do you want the people who are watching you to see? Don't you want them to see something positive that makes a lasting difference in their lives? I certainly do. I want to live my life in such a way that I leave something for others that will last forever. What I'm talking about, of course, is Jesus! In 1 Corinthians 11:1, Paul says simply, "Imitate me, just as I also imitate Christ" or "Follow my example, as I follow the example of Christ" (NIV). The big challenge is this: *I want to make sure that the people watching me see the person I'm watching. I want anybody who is following me to end up following the one I'm following – Jesus.*

> You have only one lifetime to live, but your legacy of influence for Christ can last for generations.

You have only one lifetime to live, but your legacy of influence for Christ can last for generations. Billy Graham said, "The legacy we leave is not just in our possessions, but in the quality of our lives." One day we will give an account to the Lord we follow for the lives we lead and the legacy we leave.

Kids Want to Be Like Their Heroes

When I was a kid in the eighth grade, I was watching Joe Namath. I wanted to be just like that great quarterback of the New York Jets. I mean, he was so good and he had such a great arm. He would take the ball and drop back about fifteen yards and just stand there like a Greek god. And when he threw the football, he would really throw it!

One day I picked up a copy of *Sports Illustrated* that had Joe Namath on the cover. His helmet was off, his hair was messed up, and his uniform was all dirty. He looked like a warrior in the middle of a battle. So cool! I also noticed in the picture that the middle fingers on his left hand were taped together with two strips of white tape. Maybe he had a small injury or the tape was there to keep the ball from slipping out of his hands. It didn't matter to me. I thought it was the coolest thing I'd ever seen. So the next day at practice I taped the middle fingers of my left hand just like Joe in the picture. At that time in my life I would have traded places with Joe Namath in a heartbeat. I wanted to do what he did, have what he had, and just live the life he lived.

But you know what? In time it dawned on me that those big-time athletes didn't really have what I wanted. They were cool and famous and rich, but they didn't have what I was coming to realize was most valuable. I'm talking about a life of integrity, character and godliness. I'm talking about a meaningful marriage where a man and a woman save themselves for each other and then live a lifetime together in a Christ-centered, God-honoring way. I'm talking about a husband and wife who raise godly kids to love Jesus and who are committed to a life of purity and holiness, serving Him and making a difference.

All of this changed my mind about who I wanted to imitate and follow. I realized that the person I most wanted to be like was my dad! I saw in Dad a man who loved Jesus Christ with all his heart, soul, mind and strength and who loved his wife and family faithfully. He wasn't rich or famous, but he lived a life of significance that influenced others positively. My dad became and remained my biggest hero.

Your Family Is Watching

Your family is watching you and imitating you just like I watched and imitated my dad. If you are a mom or a dad, you have kids who are watching you. If you are a student in high school or college, you have classmates, brothers, sisters, and cousins who are watching you. If your kids are grown with families of their own, you have grandchildren watching you. No matter what your role in the family is, there are people who are watching how you live and imitating you in some ways. You may not realize it, but you are a hero to others who want to be just like you. What kind of legacy are you leaving to family members who are watching and copying your example?

Someone has said that the only thing God can use to make a man is a *boy*. I think there's a lot of truth in that. If you're a man, I believe God wants to use you to show the boys in your family – sons, grandsons, younger brothers and cousins – what it means to be a real man. We can also say it this way: the only thing God can use to make a woman is a *girl*. If you're a woman, God wants you to be an example to the little girls in your family as to what a godly woman looks like.

Don't get me wrong. I know that boys need a positive influence from loving moms, grandmothers, and big sisters; and girls need strong, caring dads, granddads and big brothers in their lives. Boys need the example of women so they learn how to live with the woman they will eventually marry. And how does a young lady find the right kind of man to marry and spend her life with? Through a dad who treats her the way a young lady should be treated. Your kids are watching you. You need to set the bar high for yourself so your children grow up to be spouses and parents who are setting a proper example for those who are going to be watching them.

Where does a boy learn to love a woman the way God intends for a woman to be loved? He watches how his dad loves his mother and how his granddad loves his grandma the way God intended for a man to love a woman. I was blessed watching my dad love my mom. I learned the importance of opening doors for my wife because Dad opened doors for Mom. I taught my kids never to sass their mom because Dad would slap me upside the head whenever I sassed my mom.

There is a way that God expects a man to love his wife. It's with the same love that Jesus Christ had for His church. He literally gave himself for His church. Men, as you imitate Christ by giving yourself to nurture and care for your wives, the boys watching you will have a worthy example to follow in their own marriages. Moms, grandmas, and big sisters, the little girls in your family will learn how to love and respect their future husbands by watching how you love and respect your husband.

Where does a kid see Christ's love for us? He should see it lived out in his parents as they love each other through all the ups and downs of everyday life. Are you leaving a legacy of Christ's selfless love through your example?

A Legacy of Love for God and Country

Where do kids learn to love their country? They learn it first from parents and other family members who love their country. A little boy sees his dad and mom stand up when the flag passes during a parade. A little girl notices her dad singing the national anthem with conviction even though he can't sing a lick. Kids see older siblings signing up for military service and hear a grandfather talk about being in the military defending his country.

Where does a kid learn to love Jesus with all his heart, soul, mind and strength? From watching his parents, grandparents, and brothers and sisters love Jesus day after day, year after year. I thank God for the example of my dad and mom. They were wholeheartedly committed to Jesus Christ and to influencing others by the way they lived. I can attribute my love for Jesus to the example of my dad and mom.

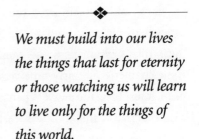

We must build into our lives the things that last for eternity or those watching us will learn to live only for the things of this world.

I'm passionate about sports. In fact, we have raised a son who is passionate about sports. And he can throw a football far better than I ever could. But if the only thing my son gets from me is a passion for throwing a football and no passion for loving Jesus Christ, then I have failed as a dad! We must build into our lives the things that last for eternity or those watching us will learn to live only for the things of this world.

A lot of people think that the best way to influence people to love Jesus Christ is by preaching to them or arguing with them. There is certainly a time and place to talk to people about Christ, but your example carries greater impact than your words. The greatest sermon about how someone can love Jesus is the *life* of someone who loves Jesus. I like the words of St. Francis of Assisi: "Preach the gospel at all times, and when necessary, use words."

You are being watched. Whether you like it or not, people are following you and imitating you and being influenced by how you live. That's one of the most powerful reasons I can think of for following Jesus and striving to be like Him. The more you are transformed into the image of Jesus, the easier it will be for you to say to those around you as Paul said, "Follow me as I follow Christ."

Where does a kid learn to love the Bible? From the example of grown-ups in his family who respect, revere and love the Bible. When I was growing up, we had "family altar" in our home. Family altar was when we gathered together as a family and my dad read the Bible to us. Now when I was around junior high age, I didn't like family altar because we had to stop what we were doing, and I was usually doing something with a ball that was a lot of fun. But Dad would say, "OK, family, let's get together." And I remember him holding the Bible in his big hands and reading to us as a family. It is a powerful image in my mind remembering how much Dad loved the Bible and hearing him read it to us.

I can also remember a time when Dad and I were in the car going somewhere. He pulled out a little New Testament, handed it to me, and said, "Neal, turn to Romans 8 and check me on this." Then he quoted to me the whole chapter – all thirty-nine verses – as we were driving down the street. I mean, it just blew me away! When my dad did those kinds of things, it instilled in me that maybe this book was worth reading, worth knowing, worth studying, worth memorizing, and worth treasuring in my heart. My dad's example is a very big reason why I am a teacher of the Bible today.

Where does a kid learn to pray? All my life I was blessed by a dad who prayed for me and with me. He would call me on the phone when I was away at college just to have a father-son conversation, and often he would say, "Hey, son, let me pray for you." Then he'd pray for me right over the phone. When I was a rookie in San Diego Chargers' training camp, Dad would send me letters nearly every day saying, "Just want you to know that I mentioned your name to the Father this morning." How powerful is that? It was like listening in as my dad prayed for me!

The Gospel of Luke mentions a few times when the disciples looked around and couldn't find Jesus. Luke tells us that they found Him praying. I can imagine Peter going out to look for Him, maybe walking around a corner or looking between some trees and rocks. Then he spots Jesus on his knees and hears Him praying to the Father. And what if Peter gets close enough to hear Jesus mention his name in prayer? Can you imagine the impact it would have on Peter's life? Jesus' praying made such a big impact on His disciples that the only thing they asked their Master to teach them was "Lord, teach us to pray" (Luke 11:1). Maybe they went on to say something like, "We've seen You pray and we've heard You pray, and we want to know how to pray just like You pray." Where would a kid develop that kind of love and respect for prayer? One place it should happen is in the family as that kid sees and hears the most important adults in his life praying for him and with him.

Where does a kid learn to love the church? Probably from parents, grandparents, brothers and sisters who attend church faithfully and pour their lives into service through the church. If it's important to you that your kids be active in the church, they must see you active in church.

Our family was at church every time the doors were open – Sundays, Wednesdays, visitation nights, special services and events. I wasn't always happy about it because it interfered with sports. As soon as Sunday lunch was over, I would head out into the neighborhood because there was always a bunch of kids ready to play ball. We would play through the afternoon and have the best time. Then Dad would show up and say, "Neal, it's time to go to church." What a bummer! I would drag into the house and spray on a little deodorant just in time to get into the car to leave for Sunday night church. Driving down the street I would look out the window and see all my friends still playing ball. I just hated it. But you know what? Today, I value the fact that I was taken to church and raised to love church.

An Example of Living and Dying

How does a kid learn to live the right way? I learned it by watching my parents. I witnessed their integrity, honesty, and character, their ability to say to each other, "I'm sorry, I was wrong." I watched my dad hug my mom and apologize when he had said something wrong or used a harsh tone of voice. You know how powerful it is for a kid to see his parents admit to each other when they are wrong and ask forgiveness? I can't tell you how many times I approach situations in life and deal with them the same way I saw my parents deal with them. I praise God for godly parents who lived godly lives in front of me, because that's how I learned to live.

My dad was raised by a wonderful Christian mother and an alcoholic father. My dad's dad was great guy, but at times he would go off on drunken binges and be gone for days. Nobody would even know where he was. When he was off drinking, my grandmother would never allow any door in the house to be locked. She wanted to make sure that when he decided to come home he would have no trouble getting into the house day or night. Well, one day my grandfather went off on a drunk and my dad never saw him again. He just never came home. For the rest of his life my dad hoped and prayed that something would happen and he would get to see his dad again. But he never did.

You know, since my dad was raised in the home of an alcoholic, it's possible that he could have become an alcoholic. Alcoholism seems to get passed from generation to generation. And if my dad had followed in his father's footsteps and become an alcoholic, it's conceivable that I could have been raised in the home of an alcoholic and that my kids could have suffered the same way. My grandfather's alcoholism could have affected my dad's life, my life, my kids' lives and generations to come.

But when my dad was a sophomore at Baylor University, something wonderful happened. He trusted Jesus Christ as his Savior, and it totally changed the direction of his life! It changed how he lived, how he loved and who he married. He married the finest woman outside of my own wife that I've ever known: my mom, Frances White. Dad's conversion changed how he raised us. Because of my dad's example, the chain of alcoholism was broken in our family and for everyone who followed.

How does a kid learn to die with honor and dignity? The best way is to watch the godly adults in his family face their own deaths with honor and dignity. My dad was only fifty-nine when he was diagnosed with pancreatic cancer. The doctors gave him three months to live, but Dad lived for a year and a half. I had watched a good and godly man live a life worthy of imitation. But when his time came to suffer, he suffered well. I watched. And when his time came to die, he died well – always positive, never complaining. I watched. He trusted in Jesus with all his heart and soul all the way to the end. I watched. He loved his wife all the way to the end. I watched. He was a witness for Jesus Christ all the way to the end. I watched. I know how a godly man lives and how a godly man dies. Because I watched one.

My mom and dad were my greatest heroes, and I wanted to be just like them. By following my parents, I ended up following the person they were following, and thank God they were following Jesus.

Theologian and medical missionary Dr. Albert Schweitzer said, "Example is not the main thing in influencing others. It is the only thing." Our daily prayer should be – "Lord Jesus, I want to be like You because so many people are watching me and following my example. I want to

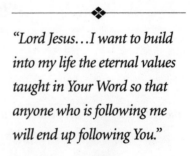

"Lord Jesus…I want to build into my life the eternal values taught in Your Word so that anyone who is following me will end up following You."

build into my life the eternal values taught in Your Word so that anyone who is following me will end up following You."

You have probably discovered that the journey of pursuing our dreams and living out God's plans is not always a pleasure cruise. The road is full of bumps, potholes, and other hazards and dangers. An important part of the journey is learning how to respond to all the negatives that threaten to stop us in our tracks. In the next section, we're going to get to the heart of this issue.

III

THE POSITIVES ABOUT NEGATIVES
How to View and Value Your Difficulties
and Defeats

Blessed is the man who perseveres under trial, because when he has stood the test,
he will receive the crown of life that God promised to those who love him.
JAMES 1:12 (NIV)

Obstacles cannot crush me. Every obstacle yields to
stern resolve. He who is fixed to a star does not change his mind.
LEONARDO DAVINCI

8

Comeback Wins Are the Greatest

There was a Texas farmer who owned an old mule, and one day his mule fell down into a dried-up well. The farmer heard braying coming from the bottom of the well, but he couldn't figure out how to haul the animal out. He was sad to think of losing such a good working mule. But since he couldn't get the mule out, the farmer brought in a truckload of dirt to bury the mule and put him out of his misery.

When the first shovels of dirt hit the old mule's back, he panicked. But as the dirt kept coming, this smart Texas mule had a thought: shake the dirt off my back and step up on it. So that's what he did. *Shake it off and step up,* he thought with each load of dirt that came down the shaft. *Shake it off and step up...shake it off and step up.* Even though the dirt falling on him was painful and frightening, he just kept shaking it off and stepping up on the mound of earth growing under his hooves. Before too long the dirt in the well got so high that the old mule stepped out and went back to work with the overjoyed farmer. The dirt that could have buried the mule actually blessed him and those around him, all because of how the mule handled his adversity.

This little story contains a big truth for those of us who seek to live out God's dreams and plans for our lives. Just like everybody else, you have things in your life that you see as negatives standing between you and your goals. Like the dirt falling on the old mule, these negatives seem to be the reasons why you can't get out of the boat or why you will surely sink and fail if you do step out. But the wise old mule quickly figured out that this negative in his life was the very thing he needed to get him out of trouble and back to work again. Once he changed his attitude about the dirt that was so painful and scary and learned to "shake it off and step up," he was on his way to freedom. In the same way, seeing the positive side of the negatives you face will help you get through them and get on with the exciting life God has for you.

Here's a powerful truth I want you to get: *God wants to use the very things you consider negatives to accomplish His big plans in your life.* He is all about turning the tears of disappointment and defeat into the thrill of victory. The key is to view these negatives as God's instruments to make you the person He wants you to be. If you want to deal with your disappointments and defeats and experience the life God has for you, you have to be positive about the negatives you face.

Lids That Hold You Down

We all have things that could be viewed as *lids* on our lives that hold us down and keep us from being what God wants us to be. While I was growing up, I saw stuttering as a lid on my life. Even as a boy, I assumed that being a stutterer would keep me from doing stuff other people who didn't stutter could do.

For example, when I went into high school in Overland Park, Kansas, I heard about this thing called student government. I thought to myself, *I need to be involved in student government. I've been involved in sports all these years, now I need to branch out, meet some new people and do some new things.* Actually, getting into student government was my dad's idea. But it was a good idea, so I decided to run for office in my sophomore class. Then I found out that if I wanted to be elected to student government, I had to stand up and make a speech to my entire class. Suddenly, I felt a big lid snap down over me and my good idea. There were nearly a thousand students in my sophomore class at

Shawnee Mission South High School. I had a severe stuttering problem, so there was no way I was going to make a speech to a thousand kids without turning it into a huge, embarrassing disaster. I wanted to give that speech, but because of my stuttering I didn't think I could pull it off. So I didn't even try! I simply decided, "I can't go there, I can't be that, and I can't do that." Now that's what I call a "lid"!

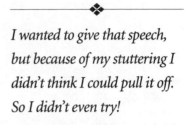

I wanted to give that speech, but because of my stuttering I didn't think I could pull it off. So I didn't even try!

Like everyone else, you have some lids that are keeping you from doing things you would like to do. Our lids are not the kind of things we like to talk about; they may be embarrassing and we'd rather keep them a secret. But if I could get you to take a sip of truth serum, you would tell me about a lid or two that have blocked you from doing what you really want to do.

You know what's amazing? We are very aware of our own lids, but we don't think other people have lids at all. You walk into a room where everybody looks good, smells good and acts confident, and you say to yourself, *She's got it all together and doesn't have anything holding her back, and that guy over there looks cool and totally in control. I must be the only one here with lids.* But the fact is — everybody is dealing with something that tends to hold them down or block their forward progress.

What kind of lids am I talking about? Well, some people see themselves limited by their *disabilities,* just as I saw stuttering as a disabling lid on my life. Other people live with *disadvantages* such as poverty or lack of education. *Disappointments* and *defeats* are huge lids that people allow to hold them down. I mean, who really likes to get up off the floor after being knocked down or turned away? We all have to deal with negatives in the pursuit of our dreams, whether they are disabilities, defects, disease, disadvantages, disappointments, defeats, disaster, or the devil himself. The challenge is how you will view and respond to these potential lids.

Get Up and Get Going

A little boy found a cocoon in his backyard and could see something moving inside, so he decided to watch it carefully. Before long a tiny hole opened in the cocoon, and the boy watched for several hours as a butterfly tried to force its way out. It seemed to be stuck. So the little boy ran into the house, got a pair of scissors, and snipped the hole wider. But when the butterfly came out, something was wrong. Its body was swollen and its wings were shriveled. It couldn't fly and soon died.

What the little boy didn't know was that the cocoon wasn't there to trap the butterfly inside. It was there by design to be a challenge. As a butterfly labors to open a hole and squeeze out, the fluid in its body is forced into its wings so the butterfly can fly. A butterfly will never fly unless it pulls itself with great effort through that little opening.

...a trouble-free life doesn't allow us to build the character and fortitude we need to reach our dreams.

Your attitude toward the lids in your life must be the same as a butterfly's attitude toward the cocoon. These negatives are not there to hold you down; they are there to make you stronger. Whatever defeats or disasters or disabilities stand between you and God's great plans for you, they are there to build you up and make you stronger. An old English proverb says, "A smooth sea never made a skilled mariner." In the same way, a trouble-free life doesn't allow us to build the character and fortitude we need to reach our dreams.

There are thousands of examples of this in the world of sports. I've read story after story of athletes who experienced a great defeat or faced an impossible challenge that actually made them come back and be more successful. There's something about being knocked down and getting back up again that makes a great athlete even greater. The only way you get to the championship is by getting up after all the knockdowns and defeats.

The man who won the decathlon gold medal in the 1952 Olympic Games was named Bob Mathias. He beat a guy named Milt Campbell in a very close competition. Do you know who won the decathlon gold medal four years later? Milt Campbell, who narrowly beat a man named Rafer Johnson. And who won the gold medal in 1960? Right, Rafer Johnson. Campbell and Johnson both won the gold after being beaten four years earlier. Getting knocked down seems to trigger an impulse and resolve for a championship effort.

I read an incredible story about a Hungarian soldier who became a championship marksman. In 1938, Sgt. Karoly Takacs was a member of Hungary's pistol shooting team. But one day during army maneuvers, a defective grenade exploded and completely shattered Takacs' right hand – his shooting hand. The whole country mourned their great champion's misfortune, knowing he could never compete again. But after a month in the hospital, Takacs picked up his pistol and quietly taught himself how to shoot all over again, this time with his left hand. In 1939, he surprised his country and the world by winning the national pistol-shooting championship.

Everyone expected Takacs to compete in the 1940 Olympics, but the 1940 and 1944 Games were cancelled because of World War II. Takacs' chance for Olympic glory had to wait until 1948. When thirty-eight-year-old Karoly Takacs arrived in London to compete in the 25-meter rapid fire pistol competition, most people didn't know he had resumed shooting after his accident. Using his less dominant left hand and less dominant left eye, Takacs stunned the world by winning the gold medal and setting a new world record in the event. He returned to the Olympics in 1952 and won the gold medal again. What a great comeback from tragedy!

Do you remember sprinter Michael Johnson? Michael was a Baylor guy from Dallas who dominated the 200-meter event in track and field for many years back in the early 1990s. Over a two-year period he won every race he entered. He was incredible! Everybody looked forward to the 1992 Olympic Games in Barcelona, expecting Michael Johnson to be a shoe-in for the 200-meter gold. But he got a little flu bug in Spain and wasn't 100 percent, so he lost in the semifinals – never even got to run for the gold. I heard Michael say that not qualifying for the finals was one of the greatest disappointments of his life. But he didn't stay down. He came back more focused and fired up than ever. Maybe you watched him run in the '96 Games in Atlanta. He not only won gold in the 200 meters and set a new world record, he won the 400 as well. His tragedy in '92 was great, but his triumph in '96 was greater.

I'm not exactly sure who Cicero was, other than one of those one-name Roman guys who seemed to be big shots. Well, Cicero said this: "The greater the tragedy, the greater the triumph." His statement is true in sports, as athletes like Karoly Takacs and Michael Johnson illustrate. But his statement is also true in life. The harder you fall, the greater the glory when you bounce back. The more bitter the failure or disappointment, the sweeter the taste of your comeback.

When you fell off your bike and skinned your knee as a kid and wanted to quit, what did your parents say? "Climb back on and try again. You can do it. You'll get it." And when you got back on, you did it and you got it! And you probably challenge your own kids the same way. If you get knocked down and stay down, you don't learn anything. But if you get knocked down and get back up to try again, what happens? You conquer some things. You become more efficient in some things. You come back a little smarter, a little stronger, a little braver and a little more determined than the last time. The key to learning from your defeats is to welcome them as God's opportunities to make you higher, swifter and stronger than ever.

Where Is the Good in the Bad?

If anybody had plenty of opportunities to learn from his defeats, it was Joseph in the Bible. You remember that God had huge plans to make Joseph a ruler over his father and eleven brothers, and He revealed His plans to Joseph in a dream. But every time Joseph took a bold, faith-filled step in the direction of his dream, he got knocked flat on his back. And it kept going on for years!

It all starts out in Genesis 37. Joseph is seventeen years old and his father's favorite son. He has this great dream about ruling over his family, a dream that reflects God's plans for him. But before the chapter is half over – POW! –

Joseph and his dream take a devastating left hook! His jealous brothers sell him to a band of traveling slave traders. By the end of chapter 37, Joseph the great dreamer and favored son has been sold as a slave into the household of Potiphar, a high-ranking Egyptian army officer.

The story picks up again in Genesis 39 with Joseph getting back on his feet. The Lord is with him and grants him success; so in time, Potiphar promotes him to be manager over his entire household. It's amazing! The dream is still alive and Joseph is still in the game. He's on his way to greatness! But the good news only lasts for six verses before Potiphar's wife starts coming on to Joseph. He's a godly man and refuses every advance. But eventually, Mrs. Potiphar frames him on a false charge of sexual assault and – BAM! - Joseph's dream takes a jolting uppercut! Near the end of chapter 39, Joseph has been fired and thrown in prison. Circumstances beyond his control have decked him for the second time.

Down for the count? Not yet. Joseph is back on his feet even before the chapter ends. God is with him and grants him success again. No, he didn't get pardoned; he's still in jail. But he becomes the warden's right-hand man in charge of the whole prison. It's incredible! Then a really big break happens. In chapter 40, Joseph interprets dreams for two other prisoners who have an "in" with the number one man in Egypt, the Pharaoh. One prisoner is released and promises to put in a good word for Joseph with the Pharaoh. Joe must be thinking that this is finally God's way for him to realize his dream. But by the end of chapter 40, *WHAM!* – a smashing punch right on the button, because the guy forgets to tell Pharaoh about Joseph! Weeks pass, months pass, and Joseph is still in jail. Hey, at this point, if I'm Joseph, I'm beginning to think that I'm snake-bit and my big dream isn't going anywhere. Well, I guess that's why God chose Joseph to be Joseph instead of me.

Genesis 41 opens with Pharaoh having strange dreams that none of his advisors can interpret. Finally after two years, Joseph's fellow prisoner remembers a guy in jail who can interpret dreams. Joseph is summoned and interprets Pharaoh's dream which warns of a coming famine. Pharaoh appoints Joseph second in command in Egypt with the task of storing up grain before the famine hits. Chapters 42-47 tell the story of Joseph reuniting with his brothers when they come to Egypt to buy grain. I guess you could say they all lived happily ever after.

But here's the question: Why did Joseph have to suffer so many defeats in the process of fulfilling God's plan for his life? He answers that question in Genesis 50. Joseph's brothers who had sold him into slavery bowed down before him fearing that they were finally going to get the payback they deserved for their horrible deed. But Joseph said to them, "You meant evil against me, but God meant it for good in order to…save many people alive" (Gen. 50:20). Using 20/20 hindsight, Joseph could see that all the negatives that happened to him were God's instruments for good in his life and the lives of others.

A man known as Charles "Tremendous" Jones said, "Things don't go wrong and break your heart so you can become bitter and give up. They happen in order to break you down and then build you up so you can be all that you were intended to be." There may be times when the disappointments and knock-downs in life make you wish you could quit and start over at the beginning. Well, you can never go back and start at the beginning again, but every day can be the start of a new beginning for the rest of your life. Your attitude toward the lids in your life is the key. Instead of resisting them as your enemies, welcome them as your friends and as God's tools to make you greater in all He has for you to do.

You may wonder, "How can I view something as a 'friend' if it's hurting me and blocking me from achieving God's plans and dreams?" That's a question the next chapter will answer.

9

Finding the Best in the Worst

A very old lady looked in the mirror one morning and saw that she had only three hairs remaining on her head. But being a positive soul she said, "I think I'll braid my hair today." So she braided her three hairs and had a great day. Some days later she looked in the mirror and noticed that she had only two hairs remaining. "Hmm, two hairs. I think I'll part them in the middle today." So she parted her two hairs and had a great day.

A week or so later only one hair was left on her head. "One hair, huh?" she said. "A ponytail will be perfect." And again she had a great day. The next morning she looked in the mirror and saw that her last hair had fallen out. "Finally bald," she said to herself. "How wonderful! Now I won't have to spend all that time doing my hair!"

I don't know who wrote that little story, but I think it tells us a lot about how to respond to the limitations and defeats we face in life. Stuttering or baldness may not be a big negative in your life, but you have other situations that prompt you to say, "I don't think God can use me with this in my life." That's where I was with my stuttering. I said things like "I can't be in student government," "I can't be a public speaker," "I won't ever get married because no girl wants to marry a stutterer." I was a living example of Henry Ford's words: "If you think you can't, you're right."

I want you to see what the Bible says about the lids you think are holding you down. It says that God wants to use them to make you into the man, woman or teenager He wants you to be. And it all begins when you change your negative attitude to a positive attitude.

Be Joyful and Grow Up

James 1:2-4 states clearly that God uses the tough things in your life to stretch and grow you, but the first thing He talks about is how you *think* about these tough things. Verse 2 says, "My brethren, count it all joy when you fall into various trials." Do you realize what you just read? It says to get excited when you are knocked down or face a limitation of some kind. The word "joy" in this verse can mean anything from a cheery smile to wild, crazy, jumping-up-and-down delight. When you feel shot down, knocked down or beaten down, it's time to laugh, sing or do a happy little dance.

"Why in the world should I do that?" you ask. "My trials, knockdowns and disappointments are not joyful things." James answers your question in verses 3-4: "Knowing that the testing of your faith produces patience. But let patience have its perfect work, that you may be perfect and complete, lacking nothing." Now the word "perfect" in this verse doesn't mean sinless or mistake-free. It's talking about being mature, complete, fully developed. And it doesn't mean your physical side; it's talking about growing up inside – it's referring to your character. That's why trials are a reason for joy. Whenever you face a trial with a positive attitude, you get stronger, tougher, more patient and more mature inside.

My attitude got a real big test at the end of my rookie season with the San Diego Chargers. The team put me on waivers, which means they were offering me to any team who wanted me because they didn't have a place for me anymore. The New York Giants claimed me off waivers and signed me to a free agent contract, so I went to the Giants' training camp in the summer of 1976. But there were so many other quarterbacks in camp that I didn't get much playing time during the drills or scrimmages.

After the second week of training camp the Giants started cutting players they didn't need. Often a player was on his way to breakfast when he was told to report to the head coach's office where the big boss broke the bad news. Well, I dreaded going to breakfast; I was always looking around for a coach who might be looking for me. Sure enough, one morning an assistant coach found me before breakfast and told me to report to Coach Bill Arnsparger's office.

Coach basically said, "Neal, you are a fine young man but you're not an NFL quarterback. You're not big enough, you don't have a strong enough arm, and I don't think you can play in this league." I wasn't going to go down without a fight. "But Coach," I argued, "you don't know what I can do because I've had no chance to show my skills as a quarterback." The problem was I started crying and stuttering so badly that nothing I said came out right. It didn't matter anyway. The Giants had cut me.

I walked out of Coach's office and headed back to the dorm to pack. I was still crying and trying to pull myself together as I walked past all my former teammates. It was one of the most humiliating experiences of my whole life. I felt like a failure, I felt defeated, I felt stupid and devastated that my dream of being an NFL quarterback had just gone up in flames. On that dark day I was anything but joyful. I was convinced I should be walking to the practice field with my teammates instead of heading to the airport as a "former Giant."

*I wasn't walking away from a bitter defeat and the death of **my** dream – I was walking into the birth of **God's** dream.*

But you know what? Looking back now, I see it from a completely different perspective. I wasn't walking away from a bitter defeat and the death of *my* dream – I was walking into the birth of *God's* dream – what He ultimately wanted me to do, which was to speak, preach and be a minister. God used that experience of defeat and disappointment to shape and direct the rest of my life. If I'd only known what God had in mind that day, I would have been jumping for joy as I left the Giants' training camp.

I didn't walk into the future as a preacher right away, though. Just twenty-four hours after I arrived home from New York, I received a phone call from the San Diego Chargers. Two of their backup quarterbacks had left camp for various reasons, and they desperately needed another quarterback. They asked me to fly out to their training camp in San Diego that night, which of course I did. I was back on top of the world at the unexpected turn of events. I finished training camp as a backup quarterback, the same position I held before they put me on waivers.

The Chargers' final preseason game that year happened to be against the New York Giants and the man who had cut me two weeks earlier, Coach Bill Arnsparger. At halftime, New York was ahead 10-7. In the locker room, Chargers' Coach Tommy Prothro told me, "Jeffrey, you are playing the second half." Well, I was excited, thrilled and scared all at once. To make a long second-half story short, I threw two touchdown passes in a comeback win over the Giants, and I was named offensive player of the game and given the game ball.

It was a great thrill on the heels of the bitter disappointment of being cut by the Giants.

Everything that happens to you – especially the hard stuff – is a cause for joy because God will use it to grow you into a person of greater depth and character.

Why did God allow me to get cut by the Giants only to give me a job with the Chargers? I really don't know. But on the way to what God ultimately wanted me to do, He allowed me a small taste of NFL football success. Bottom line of the story: Everything that happens to you – especially the hard stuff – is a cause for joy because God will use it to grow you into a person of greater depth and character.

Changed to Look like Jesus

The Bible tells us that God can bring good out of anything, even the negatives in life. Romans 8:28 is a verse we often quote when facing tough times. It starts out with three encouraging words: "And we know...." Isn't it great that there are things in the Bible we can *know?* I don't have to worry about why stuttering is in my life, and you don't need to stress over the disappointments and defeats you face. Why? Because God's Word says we can *know* some things about our struggles. And here's what we know: "We know that all things work together for good to those who love God, to those who are the called according to His purpose" (Romans 8:28). Now it's great to know that all the bad stuff in your life works together for good, but don't you want to know what the "good" is? What good thing is God getting done when so many of the "all things" are painful or unpleasant?

The next verse tells us what the good is: "For whom He foreknew, He also predestined to be conformed to the image of His Son" (v.29). The good thing God is working out through the bad and the ugly that happens to you is to conform you to the image of His Son. In other words, He is at work in "all things" to make you more like Jesus. That's not just good, that's great! You don't really learn much about yourself when things are going well. But when you get knocked down by hard circumstances and tough problems, you find out what you're made of – and so does everybody else. Plutarch, another one of those wise one-name Roman guys, said it this way, "The measure of a man is the way he bears up under misfortune."

All my life I've asked God, "Why do I have to stutter? Why does it have to be me? And why does it have to be stuttering? Why can't my trial be big ears or a big nose?" (Come to think of it, I've got those too!) "And why *now* instead of later when I'm a senile old man talking gibberish that nobody can understand anyway?" Do you know how God answers me? "Why you, Neal? Because you're the one I want to conform to My image. I want to do some things *in* you and *through* you just the way you are. Why stuttering? Because stuttering is the thing I want to use to make you strong and mature inside. And why now? Now is always the perfect time to begin because I'm ready to do amazing things right now!"

Paul says that enduring all things makes us look more like Jesus. But what does it mean to conform to His image? It's the same thing James was talking about: growing to maturity inside, in our character, so that we think and speak and respond more like Jesus. For example, Matthew 9:36 says, "But when [Jesus] saw the multitudes, He was moved with compassion for them because they were weary and scattered, like sheep having no shepherd." Perhaps a lid in your life is there because Jesus wants you to develop more of His compassion for people around you who are hurting. Or perhaps He is working on your endurance, shaping you to be more like Him "who for the joy that was set before Him endured the cross" (Hebrews 12:2).

Even if you never figure out this side of heaven exactly what God is up to in the defeats and disappointments you face, trust Him and count it all joy! He's God, and He's doing something special in you as you accept these negatives as good things from Him.

Power from an Unexpected Source

If anyone knew about lids in his life, the Apostle Paul did. Only he called his lid a "thorn." He talks about it in 2 Corinthians 12:7-10, starting with, "Lest I should be exalted above measure by the abundance of the revelations, a thorn in the flesh was given to me, a messenger of Satan to buffet me, lest I be exalted above measure" (v.7). Basically, he's saying that his thorn in the flesh was given to keep him from getting proud and cocky. Paul had experienced some important insights into the spiritual realm, maybe more than any other human being has ever seen. So to keep Paul's attitude humble like Christ's, God allowed some kind of difficulty in his life to keep him humble and dependent. What was Paul's "thorn in the flesh"? Nobody knows for sure because the Bible doesn't tell us. Maybe it was stuttering. I can tell you from experience that stuttering works wonders to humble a guy.

Paul goes on, "Concerning this thing I pleaded with the Lord three times that it might depart from me" (v.8). This verse helps me understand why people call him *Saint* Paul. I mean, he asked God to take away his thorn only three times! I'll bet I've asked God to take away my stuttering 10,000 times!

Now look at what God says to him – and to you and me: "My grace is sufficient for you, for My strength is made perfect in weakness" (v.9). Paul is quick to respond, "Therefore, most gladly I will rather boast in my infirmities, that the power of Christ may rest upon me. Therefore, I take pleasure in my infirmities, in reproaches, in needs, in persecutions, in distresses, for Christ's sake. For when I am weak, then I am strong" (vv.9-10).

Can you grasp what Paul is saying here? I mean, this is huge! He's saying that our areas of weakness are what God uses to display His power in our lives. In other words, if I don't have any weaknesses, there is no room in my life for God to show His power. Paul is claiming, "I would rather have this thorn in my life and the power of God that comes with it than to be thornless and powerless!" Billy Graham said,

Adversity is good because that's when God's power can show up to change you and change your world through you. If your weakness is a platform for God's power to be seen, then more power to Him!

"Comfort and prosperity have never enriched the world as much as adversity has." Adversity is good because that's when God's power can show up to change you and change your world through you. If your weakness is a platform for God's power to be seen, then more power to Him!

Broken to Be Used

The only way some people become who God wants them to be is for them to be broken. When life is going well – the family is healthy, the bills are paid, no tragedies, no diseases – it's easy to forget God and coast along on your good fortune. But when God allows unpleasant things to happen – you lose your job, your parents get divorced, the doctor wants to do additional tests, you total the car – you discover that God is all you really have and you desperately need Him. As Walt Disney once said, "You may not realize it when it happens, but a kick in the teeth may be the best thing in the world for you." When bad things happen, you are being challenged to cling to God and trust Him for the God-sized things only He can do.

That's what stuttering does for me. I saw it as a thorn, but then I realized it's really not a thorn at all – it's a rose – a gift that reminds me every moment how much I need Jesus in my life. Anything that reminds you of your need for Jesus is not a bad thing, but an incredible gift, a wonderful thing, something to get excited about! So why does God have to break us or stick us with thorns to get us to the point of depending on Him and letting Him work in our lives? All I know from the Bible, church history, the experiences of others, and my own experience is that God has to break us in order to transform us and use us. That just seems to be God's way of doing supernatural things. And that's why we need to receive them as gifts in a spirit of joy and thankfulness.

We often think that God can't use us for His purposes when we are struggling through trials or tragedy. We feel disqualified until we "get it all together." But God specializes in using anybody at anytime for any of His good purposes, as the next chapter will further reveal.

10

God Can Use Anybody

George was a wild, out-of-control teenager. He drank and partied big time, hung out with gangs, stole, gambled and served time in jail. If George had been in your class in high school, he might have been voted "most likely to drink himself to death" or "most likely to get shot in a gang fight." This guy was careening down the highway of self-destruction.

When George got into college, he kept up his wild living. Then one day a fellow student invited him to a Bible study. George started attending the meetings regularly and reading the Bible. One day he fell to his knees and turned his life over to God, and it totally changed his life. He dumped his bad habits and left the wild life behind. This George I'm talking about – George Mueller – went on to finish college back in the 1820s in the kingdom of Prussia, modern day Germany. Then Jesus called him "out of the boat," and he left home to become a preacher in England.

Mueller and his wife are best known for their ministry to children in the city of Bristol, England. They noticed that nothing was being done to care for the many wild, homeless street kids in town, kids who were growing up just like George did. So the Muellers took orphans into their home, and when they ran out of space, they started building orphanages where these boys and girls could be housed, fed, educated and loved. By 1870, they had established five orphanages that cared for more than 2,000 homeless kids. As a result of this couple's dream to rescue disadvantaged kids, the lives of tens of thousands of boys and girls were saved and transformed.

Here's the point: *If God can do miraculous things through a former thief, gambler, and jailbird like George Mueller, He can do miraculous things through you, no matter what your disadvantages or background may be.* This is what happens when you take a positive attitude toward the negatives in your life.

God Can Do Anything through You

Knowing what you know about yourself, what chance do you think you have of becoming a life-changing instrument of God's power like George Mueller and his wife? You may be tempted to answer, "Not much of a chance for me because…" and then state the big negatives that you think disqualify you. Maybe it's a troubled past like Mueller's. Maybe it's a physical disability like my stuttering. Maybe it's a long history of trying to be God's person and coming up short in your own eyes. But if you write yourself off because of the negatives in your life, you will miss the wonderful things God wants for you.

You see, a lot of teens and adults think that God is interested in working only through people who are nice, educated, talented, spiritually mature, experienced and out of debt. But think about it: The Bible is full of people that God used in dramatic and miraculous ways who don't fit that description. The great Apostle Paul was once a Jewish thug and hit man, terrorizing Christians and handing them over to be executed. Peter and John started out as uneducated fishermen. Matthew was a hated Jewish tax collector for the Roman government. David was an adulterer and a murderer.

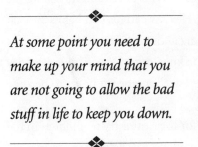

At some point you need to make up your mind that you are not going to allow the bad stuff in life to keep you down.

At some point you need to make up your mind that you are not going allow the bad stuff in life to keep you down. That you're going to be faithful to Jesus no matter what. You're going to keep believing Him, and you're going to bravely face all the difficult situations that come along. God can work with this kind of attitude big time! If you remain faithful, He can do something through you that will touch your world. And the world will see you as someone who is less than perfect but "more than a conqueror" as you keep trusting Jesus.

There's a great story in the Bible about God doing miraculous things in a potentially disastrous situation through people who simply trusted Him. In Daniel 3, the conquered Jews were living in the land of Babylon where they had been exiled. King Nebuchadnezzar of Babylon built a golden statue nearly 100 feet tall and then demanded that everyone bow down to it. How serious was he? Anyone who didn't worship the big idol would be thrown into a blast furnace and burned alive! That's how serious!

Well, there were three bright and talented Jewish guys named Shadrach, Meshach and Abednego who served in the king's court. They said to each other, "Hey, we can't bow down to this idol because we serve the one true God. We've got to stand up for our God and honor Him even if we end up toast." Literally! So they stood tall when everyone else dropped to their knees in front of the golden statue. Sure enough, they got busted, tried and sentenced to death in the furnace.

If I'd happened to be one of those guys, I would have been praying up a storm. "Why me, God? And why this? I've got my whole life ahead of me. I can be a good witness for you here in pagan Babylon. But how can you do anything good with me if I get roasted like a hot dog?"

Shadrach, Meshach and Abednego may have wrestled through questions like these, but they made the tough call and "got out of the boat." They stood up for their God and trusted Him for the results. Their conviction and obedience under fire remind me of John Maxwell's words: "A difficult time can be more readily endured if we retain the conviction that our existence holds a purpose – a cause to pursue, a person to love, a goal to achieve."

When the king gave the three boys a last chance to bow down before the idol, they said, "We have no need to answer you in this matter...Our God whom we serve is able to deliver us from the burning fiery furnace, and He will deliver us from your hand, O king. But if not, let it be known to you, O king, that we do not serve your gods, nor will we worship the gold image which you have set up" (Daniel 3:16-18).

Did you catch that? They said that God was able to get them through the fire unhurt. But they also knew that God might *not* deliver them! They knew that God would do whatever He purposed to do, so they purposed to stand up for Him no matter what happened. It's the same faith that Peter showed when he climbed out of the boat not knowing if he would end up on *top* of the water or *under* the water.

Well, the boldness of the three Hebrew boys really ticked off the king. He cranked up the heat in the furnace by 700 percent and gave the go-ahead for the execution. The fire was so hot that the guards who threw them in were vaporized in the heat. Then King Neb got himself a ringside seat to watch the rebellious Jewish boys get burned to ashes.

Check this out:

> *The king was astonished; and he rose in haste and spoke, saying to his counselors, "Did we not cast three men bound into the midst of the fire?"*
>
> *They answered and said to the king, "True, O king."*
>
> *"Look!" he answered, "I see four men loose, walking in the midst of the fire; and they are not hurt, and the form of the fourth is like the Son of God."* (Daniel 3:24-25)

Do you see what happened here? Because these three guys stood up and did the right thing in a difficult situation, a pagan king saw what many think was the appearance of Jesus Christ in the midst of the flames – that He was the *fourth* man in the furnace. That's the whole idea. When you have a positive attitude toward your disappointments and defeats and stand up for God and trust Him anyway, other people will see Christ in your life!

When bad things happen to you and you remain true to Jesus Christ and face your trial with faith, courage, and even joy, the world looks on and says, "Whoa! What a great attitude! The God she serves must be a great God." Or if you're just an average person with an average life who is remaining faithful to God through the average ups and downs of life, people can look at you and say, "There's nothing particularly special about that guy, but God is using him in an amazing way. There must be something special about his God."

You know why I want to be faithful to Jesus in both the good times and bad times, when life is smooth and when things get bumpy? Because ultimately, I want my son and daughters, their spouses and kids, the people in my church, the people I work with and the people in my neighborhood to say, "All that Jesus stuff Neal talks about must be for real. I can see Jesus in his life no matter what happens to him. I'm convinced that Jesus Christ is worth my life and my all."

No Guarantees

Not every experience of trusting God and standing up for Him against great odds has a storybook ending like it did for Shadrach, Meshach and Abednego. Sometimes God makes the negatives go away; sometimes He doesn't. Our call is to trust Him and let Him work through us whether things turn out the way we want or not. He will use us anyway, with or without our lids.

Consider John the Baptist. Jesus said he was a greater prophet than Elijah, and God used John to introduce Jesus to the world. But when John was thrown into prison because of his stand for the truth, he didn't get out. He was beheaded. Jesus could have stopped it if He had chosen to, but He didn't. Why not?

Acts 12:6-11 tells the great story of an angel springing the Apostle Peter from prison where he's about to be executed for his faith. But in the first five verses of that chapter, King Herod kills the Apostle James with the sword because of his faith. Both Peter and James are standing tall for Jesus, but one gets cut down and one goes free. Tradition says that ten of the original twelve disciples – as well as the Apostle Paul – were eventually martyred for their faith. What's up with that?

When you step out of your comfort zone and trust God to work through you, He'll do it. But He doesn't guarantee what we might call a "happy ending" in this lifetime. Jesus said, "…He makes His sun rise on the evil and on the good, and sends rain on the just and on the unjust" (Matthew 5:45). When we step out of the boat in response to Jesus' invitation, we can expect to get wet as He uses us according to His will. No wonder Paul wrote about Christ being "magnified in my body, whether by life or by death" (Philippians 1:20). And the apostle issues the same invitation to us: "I beseech you therefore, brethren, by the mercies of God, that you present your bodies a living sacrifice, holy, acceptable to God, which is your reasonable service" (Romans 12:1).

When we present ourselves to God as living sacrifices, the happy ending is that He works through us to accomplish His purposes. When God is directing your life, He may deliver you from some negative stuff – and that will bring Him glory – but He may also *leave* you in negative stuff and still accomplish His ultimate will through it.

Glory, Glory Hallelujah!

When you trust God in the middle of your trials, He works *in* you and He works *through* you to accomplish great things, even miraculous things. But there's something else that happens when you have a positive, trusting attitude toward trials – God receives glory through it all.

Look at what happened after Shadrach, Meshach and Abednego stepped out of the furnace without even their clothes smelling like smoke. The king was blown away and said, "Blessed be the God of Shadrach, Meshach and Abednego, who sent His angel and delivered His servants who trusted in Him" (Daniel 3:28). Later the king wrote, "I thought it good to declare the signs and wonders that the Most High God has worked for me. How great are His signs, and how mighty His wonders! His kingdom is an everlasting kingdom, and His dominion is from generation to generation" (Daniel 4:2-3). This was a pagan king giving glory to God. That's incredible! He was telling everybody about the great God of the Hebrews.

Now what if those three Jewish boys had caved in and bowed down to the idol to save their own hide? Well, I can think of two things that wouldn't have happened. First, King Nebuchadnezzar would *not* have seen God walking with the young men in the flames; and second, God would not have received glory through the king's testimony. But Shadrach, Meshach and Abednego did remain faithful to God, and He received glory through the miracle they experienced.

Here's what I want you to see: *God can get the glory through everything you endure as long as you remain faithful to Him.* He gets the glory if I win the championship and give Him praise for it, and He also gets the glory if I finish dead last, yet honor Him in the effort. He gets glory if I live a long life of sacrificial service to Him, and He gets the glory if I suffer and die young with a strong testimony. In fact, the greater the tragedy I experience as I serve Jesus Christ, the greater the triumph in the glory He receives.

You don't have to look very far in the Bible to see how God can bring triumph and glory out of tragedy. The greatest tragedy the world has ever known happened on Good Friday when Jesus Christ was crucified on the cross. Humanly speaking, it was the worst imaginable thing on earth that could have happened. Here is the Creator of the universe, born on this planet to save us from our sins, and yet He was betrayed, arrested, illegally tried, severely beaten, mocked, spit on and crowned with thorns.

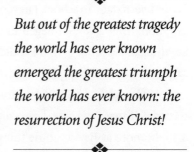

But out of the greatest tragedy the world has ever known emerged the greatest triumph the world has ever known: the resurrection of Jesus Christ!

Then He was nailed to a cross to die with the weight of the whole world's sin on His shoulders. But out of the greatest tragedy the world has ever known emerged the greatest triumph the world has ever known: the resurrection of Jesus Christ!

This reality should fire you up with hope! You will never suffer a trial or defeat or loss or difficulty as great as Jesus suffered. Are you disabled because of disease or injury, struggling with some kind of handicap, being made fun of at school, recovering from the death of a loved one, being criticized for your faith, or devastated by financial ruin? As difficult as these things are to deal with, they're not even close to the tragedy of Jesus' crucifixion! That's why you can have such great hope. If God can transform the tragedy of the crucifixion into the greatest triumph of all time, what great victory might God want to bring out of your negative circumstances?

I'm Gonna Start Talking!

It took more than forty years for me to see my tragedy of stuttering as a reason for joy instead of despair. My greatest fear was being seen and known as a stutterer. I was ashamed of how I talked and sounded when I messed up words. I was embarrassed by how I looked when I stuttered. I've watched myself on video and it's ugly, not just the words, but the blinking and the faces I make trying to get the words out. I just hate seeing myself stutter through a talk.

My number one objective for most of my life was to hide the fact that I stuttered. But the only way I could do that was to never talk, so I did everything I could *not* to talk. In school, I never raised my hand in class to answer a teacher's question. After a while I began to think that maybe I was stupid. I never said anything in class, but even if I could say something, I didn't know what I would say. I was just so ashamed all the time.

William Ward said, "Adversity causes some men to break, others to break records." If that's the case, I grew up broken by my stuttering. But when I was a sophomore at Baylor, some things happened that brought me to a turning point. I knew God had called me to be a preacher, which seemed pretty impossible for a guy who stutters. But as a Christian athlete at Baylor, I kept getting these invitations from churches around Central Texas to come and share my testimony. My response was always to come up with excuses as to why I couldn't accept those invitations.

But God had other ideas. He used the miraculous incident of fluent speech in Lubbock to show me that He could stop me from stuttering if He chose to, even though that's the only time He chose to. Then He kept opening doors for me to speak at churches. The message was becoming clearer to me. God wanted me to preach. I had opportunities to preach, and He could use me when I spoke, whether I stuttered or not. And Sheila – my girlfriend at the time, and now my wife – just happened to be a speech therapist; so she encouraged me and helped me through all of this. Finally, one day I realized I could no longer say no to what God was calling me to do. So I decided, "I'm going to stand up and start talking even if everybody laughs at me. I've got something to say and I'm going to start saying it! I'm going to accept speaking invitations even though they are horrifying experiences for me."

Do you know what happened when I made that decision? My whole life changed! Not because I stopped stuttering, because I didn't stop. My life changed when my attitude toward my stuttering changed! I realized that the challenge is not about exercising my gifts to be a great talker, because I'm anything but a great talker. It's about my answering God's call to give all I could give to become all I could be. I had to get out of the boat

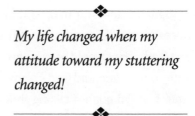

My life changed when my attitude toward my stuttering changed!

and trust Him to work in me and through me to bring Him glory in spite of my stuttering. And that's just what He's done. I still stutter. I still blink a million times and make weird faces when I talk. I still get laughed at occasionally. But God has taken my weakness and used it to change lives. And because God has done it, He gets all the glory. My stuttering is no longer *my* problem – it's *His* problem. If He wants to use me this way, more power to Him because He can do anything He wants to do.

When my attitude toward stuttering changed, I began to see it not as a problem but as a possibility that was precious. It is precious to me because God has chosen to do a few good things through me even though I stutter. He has taken something I considered to be ugly and actually made it beautiful, lovely and precious to me because He has done beautiful, lovely and precious things through it all.

I feel the same way about my wife Sheila's scars from surgery following breast cancer. Most people might think those scars are ugly, but I think they are beautiful and precious because they mean she is alive – a breast cancer survivor. Some people might look at the scars Jesus received at the cross and say they are ugly. But those scars – the pierced hands and feet, the torn flesh from the crown of thorns, the slash in His side from the spear – are the reason I have forgiveness of sin and eternal life. Those scars remind me that He suffered and died for me, so they are beautiful and precious to me.

Do you have any scars? If so, you need to look at them the same way. Whatever about you that you consider ugly – a handicap, a defeat, a failure, or whatever – can become precious and beautiful in your eyes as you begin to rejoice in it, thank God for it, and watch Him use it in your life.

About now you may be thinking, "Scars? Thorns? Knock-downs? That doesn't sound like a very fun life to me!" Well, nobody said pursuing your dreams and God's plans would be easy. If you want to get over your negatives and get on with your dreams and God's plans, you're going to have to battle through some stuff. And I'm not just talking about working through the negatives in life. I'm talking about fighting a real enemy who wants to stop you from achieving what God wants you to achieve. In Section IV, I'm going to expose your enemy and his tactics and show you how to fight for the destiny God has for you.

IV

BATTLE FOR YOUR BEST

How to View and Value Doing the Right Thing

*For we do not wrestle against flesh and blood, but against
principalities, against powers, against the rulers of the darkness
of this age, against spiritual hosts of wickedness in the heavenly places.*

EPHESIANS 6:12

*I often laugh at Satan, and there is nothing that makes him so angry as when
I attack him to his face, and tell him that through God I am more than a
match for him.*

MARTIN LUTHER

11

Someone Wants to Take You Down

Everything has an enemy. In sports, every champion has at least one contender who would like nothing better than to kick him or her off the top rung. Everything in nature has an enemy. Every bug and bird and beast is on the menu of some critter a little higher up the food chain. It's even dog-eat-dog in the business world. Somebody in your company is probably trying right now to get promoted to your position; a rival company would like nothing better than to whittle away at your market share; a competitor is trying to lure your best customers away with low-ball pricing. The world seems driven by fierce competition and a survival-of-the-fittest mentality.

You also have some deadly enemies as you respond to Jesus' call to believe and get out of the boat. You may be committed to stand up for God and be His person in the world despite your disappointments and defeats, but someone very evil, deceitful and powerful has you in his crosshairs and is dead set on watching you sink instead of swim.

Here's the key point: *There is a war going on over what God wants to achieve through you. In order to get past the negatives and achieve God's great purpose for your life, you will have to battle an enemy who has vowed to destroy you and everything God wants to do in and through you.*

Your Enemy Wants to Destroy You

In the spiritual world, your number one enemy is Satan. The Bible calls him a thief and a liar. His objective is to rob you of the good things God wants for you. In John 10:10, Jesus tells us what Satan is up to: "The thief does not come except to steal, and to kill, and to destroy." Whatever God wants *for* you, Satan wants to take *from* you. His goal is to stomp out all the good things God stirs in your heart to do and to destroy His plans for your life.

But in the same verse, Jesus continues with the good news: "I have come that they may have life, and that they may have it more abundantly." God wants you to experience an incredible life and enjoy a close, loving relationship with Him. He wants you to experience blessed, meaningful relationships with your parents, your spouse, your kids and your friends. He also wants you to leave a mark of love and faithfulness in your world that cannot be erased, a legacy for all who come after you.

Do you know what is really sad? This thief is very successful at robbing people like you and me of things that have far greater value than money or possessions. Here are some things he is trying to steal from you:

- *Your concept of God* – Satan doesn't want you to see God as all-powerful and all-loving. He will try to convince you that God is just a senile, bewhiskered old fuddy-duddy who has no power whatsoever.
- *Your self-image* – Your enemy doesn't want you to believe in your infinite worth and value. Satan wants you to feel inadequate, always comparing yourself to how other people look, what they have, and what they do. We need to get our self-image from the one Person who is perfect and complete. God says, "I love you just as you are. You are complete, forgiven and accepted."

- *Your wholeness* – Too many people today are not whole; they are broken, bruised and defeated because the enemy has robbed them. The enemy wants us to be so anxious, addicted, dominated, divided, defeated, empty and consumed with stuff that we end up writing ourselves off as helpless and useless.
- *Your power in worship* – Have you ever felt like God wasn't interested in your worship? That's from your enemy. Whether you're a teenager, a senior adult, or in between, God loves to hear your praise and worship. Psalm 22:3 tells us that God inhabits or is enthroned in the praises of His people. He "resides" there.
- *Your sexual purity* – If Satan can get you to compromise your sexual purity, he can rob you of your close relationships and destroy your positive influence for Jesus.
- *Your family unity* – Satan will try to stir up arguments to divide your family and rob you of the family relationships and mutual support God intended for parents and children to share.
- *Your impact on others* – Your enemy will tempt you to pursue popularity, money, position and power to distract you from growing in godliness and character.
- *Your influence for Christ* – Because God wants to use you to lead people to Christ, Satan will bombard you with feelings of fear, insecurity and unworthiness in an effort to wipe out any godly influence you might have on others.

There are two vivid images in the Bible that reveal what your enemy is intent on doing to you. The first image is that of a hungry lion who wants to *devour* you. The second image is that of being *sifted* like wheat to expose your secret sins to the world.

Your Enemy Wants to Devour You

The first image is found in 1 Peter 5:8: "Be sober, be vigilant, because your adversary the devil walks about like a roaring lion, seeking whom he may devour." It's the picture of a hungry lion ready to kill and devour the first animal he can catch. Your enemy wants to tear you apart, chew you up and swallow you! He wants to destroy your relationship with God. He wants to reduce your marriage and family relationships to confusion, conflict and divorce. He wants your life dominated by things that will consume you and ultimately decimate you.

But you know what? A vicious, roaring lion cannot catch every animal he sets his mind to because many of them can outrun him. So the animal that ends up on the lion's dinner plate is usually one that is weak and vulnerable or careless. It's the same in the spiritual world. Satan can't have anybody he wants. He has to prowl around looking for someone who is weak and vulnerable. If you are walking in the power of the Holy Spirit and are protected by the armor of God, Satan can't overpower you. So he looks for somebody whose defenses are down, who left a back door open, who is hiding things in a dark corner, or is playing around with a secret sin. That's the person he will single out and pounce on.

Several years ago my wife and I were in Branson, Missouri. They have one of those big IMAX theaters with the huge screen, so we went to see a film called *Africa*. It was incredible! The photography was spectacular and that huge wrap-around screen makes you feel like you are right in the middle of the action.

One part of the film followed a herd of wildebeests migrating across the African plains. As the herd came to this narrow canyon where they had to pass through single file, a pride of lions was crouching in the crevices of the canyon walls, waiting for the exact right moment to strike. Well, the herd could see the lions, so they didn't want to go through the canyon because they knew that one of them was going to become a meal. So the wildebeests were prancing nervously at the mouth of the canyon going crazy with fear. None of them wanted to be the first to go through. Meanwhile, the lions waited patiently, licking their chops and flicking their tails.

Then suddenly it happened. In a flurry of dust, the wildebeests took off through the canyon, running single file and wild-eyed for their lives. The sound of the rumbling herd was awesome! The camera zoomed in on the wildebeests; then it showed the lions crouched, watching, waiting for the right moment, sizing up the herd, looking for the vulnerable ones who were young or old or injured or slow. Suddenly the lions sprang into action! They took off after one poor wildebeest that was slightly crippled. It tried to escape, running, dodging and kicking, but it was hopeless. The lions swarmed over it, pulled it down, dragged it off, ripped it apart and ate it. The poor wildebeest wasn't just conquered – he was devoured!

The enemy of your soul has even worse plans for you. He's just waiting for an opening when you are playing games with him instead of defending yourself against his schemes. When you make yourself vulnerable by letting down your guard, you make it easy for him to find you, capture you, and devour you spiritually, emotionally and relationally. If you have some unhealthy things in your life, some areas where you are compromising your walk with God, you're like that crippled wildebeest. You're a prime target for being pulled down and devoured.

Your Enemy Wants to Expose Your Weakness

The second Bible image of what your enemy wants to do to you is that of being sifted like wheat. The scene in Luke 22 is near the end of Jesus' earthly ministry when He is talking about being betrayed and going to the cross. Jesus says to Simon Peter, "Simon, Simon! Indeed, Satan has asked for you, that he may sift you as wheat" (v.31). Using Simon's name twice suggests that what Jesus had to say was real important. He wanted Simon Peter's full attention. I hope Jesus has your attention as He describes what your enemy Satan is all about.

The first thing Jesus tells Simon is that Satan has *asked* for him. Now when Satan asks for you, it's not a good thing. He's not asking for you because he wants to help you out or give you something nice or encourage you. We already know that he comes to steal, kill and destroy. So if Satan is asking for you, he's planning to do something that will mess you up and bring you down.

So why did Satan ask for Peter? Why didn't he just pounce on him like a hungry lion and devour him? Because he can't do anything to Simon Peter or to you without God's permission. First Corinthians 10:13 says, "No temptation has overtaken you except such as is common to man; but God is faithful, who will not allow you to be tempted beyond what you are able, but with the temptation will also make the way of escape, that you may be able to bear it." Why would God give Satan permission to tempt you in the first place? Because God wants you to mature in character, and the only way that's going to happen is through trials. Satan's attacks may be difficult and painful, but if you are walking in the Spirit and following Jesus obediently, Satan's attacks can't destroy you even though God is allowing the attack.

> *...if you are walking in the Spirit and following Jesus obediently, Satan's attacks can't destroy you even though God is allowing the attack.*

They only serve to build up your character and make you more like Jesus!

In Luke 22:31, Jesus tells Peter that Satan wants to *sift* him like wheat. What's He talking about? Well, He's referring to the way farmers separated the wheat from the chaff back in Jesus' day. The bundles of harvested wheat were taken from the field to the threshing floor. The heads of grain were beaten so that the kernels of wheat were separated from the chaff, which is the part you can't eat. Then everything was tossed into the air so the wind could blow away the chaff and let the kernels of wheat fall back to the floor where they could be gathered up.

Satan was asking to sift Peter, to separate the wheat from the chaff in his life. He wanted to expose some bad stuff in Peter, such as a weakness hidden in a dark corner of his life. It may have been buried so deep that even Peter didn't know it was there, but Satan wanted to bring it out so he could use it to destroy the great apostle.

Jesus was quick to encourage Peter in light of the trial that was coming. He said, "I have prayed for you that your faith should not fail; and when you have returned to me, strengthen your brethren" (Luke 22:32). That's incredible! Jesus allows Satan a little room to rough us up, to test us and try us. But He says, "Don't worry; I'm praying for you that your faith will tough it out during the sifting. And when you get through it, I want you to encourage others who are being sifted."

Well, Peter doesn't think Jesus has anything to worry about. He boasts, "Lord, I am ready to go with You, both to prison and to death" (v.33). But Jesus replies, "I tell you, Peter, the rooster shall not crow this day before you will deny three times that you know me" (v.34). And that's exactly what happened. In the courtyard during Jesus' trial, Peter cursed and swore and lied and denied that he knew Jesus. He had bragged about how brave he was, but when the pressure mounted, his secret fear and cowardice were exposed for all to see.

Peter got sifted, and Satan wants to sift you in the same way. He wants to put you in situations where your secret sins are exposed, where you are discredited and your reputation is ruined. He knows about the stuff you keep hidden in the dark corners of your heart, the stuff you don't want anybody to know about. He wants to bring you down by exposing your secrets. Being sifted means your colleagues know, your parents know, your spouse knows, your kids know, your friends know, and your church knows. You've kept things under wraps for a long time, but when Satan sifts you, your wraps are untied and your secrets sins are not secrets anymore.

I remember a well-known evangelist who held great crusades all around the world, but he had a secret sin in his life that continued for years. It involved pornography – the magazines, the lust, the fantasy, and all that stuff. Nobody knew about it, so he kept right on preaching in country after country. But then one day he got caught, and his secret sin was exposed. With tears rolling down his face like rain on a window pane, he stood in the pulpit of his church and confessed his sin on national television. His wife and family were there. The news media were there. In a matter of minutes, the secret he had hidden from the world was exposed to the world.

What happened to him? He got *sifted*. All that stuff nobody knew about him blew up in his face. That's what your enemy intends to do. He wants to expose your faults, your mistakes, your fears and your sins so he can destroy you with them. He says, "Look at you! You call yourself a Christian? No way! Look at all the stuff you've done. You might as well pack it in because God can't use you."

Here are two things you need to keep in mind about Satan's sifting. *First, he can find plenty of flaws in all of us.* We all make mistakes and sin. Even though at this moment nobody else knows about your sin, that addiction is exposed, that lust conceives an act, or that secret becomes public, and everything you hold dear can be seriously damaged or destroyed.

Second, don't give Satan what he needs to work with. Paul wrote, "Put on the Lord Jesus Christ, and make no provision for the flesh to fulfill its lusts" (Romans 13:14). Examine your life daily and deal with any area of potential sin. Pray with David, "Search me, O God, and know my heart; try me, and know my anxieties; and see if there is any wicked way in me, and lead me in the way everlasting" (Psalm 139:23-24). When God reveals sin in your life, repent, turn around and start going in the right direction. Dealing with sin in this way will greatly limit Satan's ability to sift you and bring you down.

You may be old enough to remember the British rock group "Queen" from thirty years ago. They had a huge hit single in 1980 called "Another One Bites the Dust." It was a hard-driving rock tune with a chorus that said, "Another one bites the dust, another one bites the dust. Another one gone and another one gone. Another one bites the dust. Hey, I'm gonna get you, too. Another one bites the dust."

The fact is, every time a man leaves his wife for another woman or a woman leaves her husband for another man or a teen falls to the temptation of sexual immorality or drugs, all the demons in hell rejoice and sing, "Another one bites the dust!" Every time a Christian makes an idol out of money or possessions, that chorus rings out again. Every time a dad or a mom forfeits a child for the sake of building a career or an empire, "Another one bites the dust!" Whenever you yield to Satan's devouring or sifting, the demons in hell have a party.

Do you realize that Satan is the mortal enemy of your soul and that his aim in life is to take you down, get you off the playing field and make you a non-factor? Your challenge every day is to identify those areas where you are being stalked and sifted by the enemy, and allow Jesus Christ to cleanse you. In the next chapter, I'll help you rise to that challenge.

12

Fatal Flaws

We've been talking about how Satan is just waiting and watching to take advantage of a flaw in your life so he can mess up God's great plans for you. You may be doing really well in a lot of areas. You read your Bible every day; you attend church regularly and give generously when the offering plate comes by; you even donate time as a volunteer in the community. You love your kids, honor your parents, and so on. Let me tell you, Satan isn't impressed with what you do. He's too busy watching for a weakness he can attack, such as a secret little sin nobody knows about, a negative thought toward somebody, a bad habit or worldly attitude. And when he finds a flaw, he intends to expose it and deal you a fatal blow. He will attack you at that weakness and try to bring you down.

Here's the big idea: *Satan won't attack you where you're strong; he will attack you where you're weak and vulnerable and careless.* You need to identify any potential fatal flaws in your life and address those areas to keep Satan from using them to destroy you.

In this chapter we're going to take a serious look at where you are in life and what is really going on in your heart. I want to identify and address areas where even a tiny flaw will open the door for Satan to attack your witness and influence for Christ, ruin your relationships with your parents, spouse and kids, and disqualify you from experiencing everything God has for you.

Beware of Fatal Flaws

The Fatal Flaw of Money. A young Jewish man walked up to Jesus one day and asked what he had to do to inherit eternal life. Jesus answered by quoting a few of the commandments, and the young man said he had kept them all since he was a boy. Here's what happened next:

> *Then Jesus, looking at him, loved him, and said to him, "One thing you lack: Go your way, sell whatever you have and give to the poor, and you will have treasure in heaven; and come, take up the cross, and follow Me." But he was sad at this word, and went away sorrowful, for he had great possessions.* (Mark 10:21-22)

Did you notice the two words "loved him"? It's great to know that when you come to Jesus, you come to someone who loves you deeply and wants what is best for you. He may ask you to do something that seems difficult, but you can be assured that He will provide a way for you to achieve what He asks you to do.

This young man had a fatal flaw that Jesus needed to point out. It was the guy's attachment to his money and all it could buy. It became a *fatal* flaw because it blocked him from knowing Jesus and enjoying eternal life. On another occasion Jesus said to his followers, "What will it profit a man if he gains the whole world, and loses his own soul?" (Mark 8:36).

Some people are missing the incredible things God has for them because money and possessions dominate their lives. They say, "I want to build my career and make the big bucks. I want a big house and everything that comes with it – the cars, the boat, the cruises, the country club membership, the whole enchilada!" The temptation can be just as great for teens whose top priority is getting all the "cool stuff" other kids have – the latest cell phones, MP3s, clothes with the right label, and so on. There's nothing wrong with money or stuff unless it's more important to you than living out God's plans for your life. That's when it becomes fatal.

My wife and I live in a suburb of Dallas, Texas, in a nice, average house. We love our place. We have a great yard with lots of grass and flowers everywhere. But let me tell you something: If God has something else He wants us to do somewhere else in the world, and we say "No thanks" because we love our house and career and stuff, it would put us in a very dangerous position. We could miss the great things God has for us. And no house, no pile of stuff, no amount of money is worth that!

One of the great secrets of life is discovering that you don't need all the stuff the world is trying to sell you on television. So if your salary or career or possessions are standing between you and following Christ, you may have too much stuff. I want to encourage you to keep a *light* grip on your possessions so you can maintain a *tight* grip on becoming who God wants you to be.

The Fatal Flaw of Pride. Pride says, "It's all about me." It shows up in our relationship with God when we think it's all about what God gives me or does for me. At home, pride says, "Mom and Dad should give me anything I want" or "My spouse and kids should plan their schedules around me." Pride is a flaw that Satan will use to keep you from experiencing God's best.

Acts 12 gives us a picture of what God thinks of pride. King Herod dressed up in his royal robe, sat on his throne, and delivered a big speech. Then look what happened: "And the people kept shouting, 'The voice of a god and not a man!' Then immediately an angel of the Lord struck him, because he did not give glory to God. And he was eaten by worms and died" (Acts 12:22-23). Herod's pride was a fatal flaw – literally! It doesn't just say he died. No, it says he was eaten by worms and then died. That's a bad way to go!

Pride is something I have wrestled with all my life. As an athlete, I kind of had this 'tude going. I'm the man. I make the team go. I make the plays. If the Baylor football team got written up in the sports pages of the Waco paper, I could scan an article and find my name in seconds. Pride pulls our eyes away from Jesus. C.S. Lewis wrote, "A proud man is always looking down on things and people; and, of course, as long as you're looking down, you can't see something that's above you."

God says, "Pride and arrogance and the evil way and the perverse mouth

I hate" (Proverbs 8:13). It's not good to do anything that God hates. Anything God hates qualifies as a fatal flaw. Your life is not all about you. It's about being God's witness in the world. It's about doing what He gives you to do. Putting yourself first will mess up your marriage, your family and your influence.

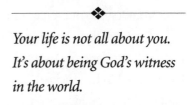

Your life is not all about you. It's about being God's witness in the world.

The Fatal Flaw of Independence. This kind of independence says, "The rules apply to everyone except me." In 2 Samuel 11, King David got into big trouble when he exempted himself from the rules. Israel was at war, but he stayed home and got trapped in lust that led to an affair with Bathsheba. Then he had her husband killed to try to cover up his sin.

David's flaws were that he was not where he should have been and was not doing what he should have been doing – leading his army in battle. Instead, he was where he should *not* have been, doing what he should *not* have been doing – sneaking around on his rooftop getting an eyeful of Bathsheba. For that, David got sifted!

You can fall into a lot of trouble when you expect other people to do the right thing, yet you allow yourself to slide in the process. For example, you would never let your kids watch certain movies or TV channels, but you fail to apply the same standard for yourself. The Bible says plainly, "To him who knows to do good and does not do it, to him it is sin" (James 4:17).

The Fatal Flaw of Busyness. In Luke 10, Jesus is visiting with his friends Mary and Martha. Mary takes full advantage of the opportunity to sit down and listen to Jesus, but Martha "was distracted with much serving" (v.40). Do you remember what Jesus said? "Martha, Martha, you are worried and troubled about many things. But one thing is needed, and Mary has chosen that good part, which will not be taken away from her" (vv.41-42).

I think Jesus' description of Martha fits a lot of people today: worried and troubled about many things. We cram our calendars full of activities and entertainment that contribute little value to our walk with Christ. It's like the hectic life described by author Jane Austen: "A quick succession of busy nothings." We let too many things get in the way of the most important thing: spending time with Him. Somebody has said, "If the Devil can't make you bad, he'll just make you busy." The flaw of busyness becomes fatal when it takes us away from Jesus as our top priority.

The Fatal Flaw of Being a People-Pleaser. When Jesus was on trial before Pontius Pilate, the crowd wanted Him dead. They kept accusing Jesus and saying He deserved to be crucified. Five times Pilate answered the people, "I find no fault in him." He said he was going to let Jesus go. But the people "were insistent, demanding with loud voices that He be crucified...So Pilate gave sentence that it should be as they requested" (Luke 23:23-24). Even though Pilate knew that Jesus was innocent and killing Him was wrong, the crowd wanted it, and he wanted to please the crowd.

All my life it has been a temptation for me to try please the people around me because I've been insecure about who I am because of my stuttering. I often think, *You're not going to like me because I stutter, so I've got to find some way to please you.* A lot of my behavior has been an effort to get people to like me and accept me. It's one of the reasons I went so far in sports. I had natural abilities, but I also worked hard to excel because I hoped people would accept me as a great athlete.

Do you realize how tragic it is when your main objective in life is to make everybody else happy? It's impossible! The secret is to discover that you really only have an audience of One, and that is God. Make it your goal to serve and honor and glorify Him. It really doesn't matter what anybody else thinks. Living to please people will take your focus away from pleasing God, and that can be fatal in so many ways.

The Fatal Flaw of Deceit. Acts 5 tells the tragic story of Ananias and Sapphira, a Christian married couple who lied and paid a huge price for it. Some members of the early church sold their property and donated the money to the church so everyone could be cared for. This couple gave only a portion of their profits – which was no problem – except they deceived everyone by saying they had given the full amount. For them it was really a fatal flaw, and God struck them both dead.

Have you ever tried to appear more godly or spiritual than you really are? It's easy to do. Just drop a phrase like, "I had a wonderful quiet time with the Lord this morning" or "I'm memorizing the book of Deuteronomy." Everybody will think, "Whoa! What a great Christian!" But if you are exaggerating the truth to impress people, that's deceit and, as Ananias and Sapphira found out, it's serious. Satan can use this fatal flaw to destroy your credibility and your witness for Christ.

As a Christian guy in high school, college, and even in seminary, I was more interested in making people think I knew Jesus Christ than I was in actually knowing Jesus Christ. If I had spent as much time pursuing my relationship with the Lord as I did trying to convince people I was pursuing the Lord, I would have had a much more intimate and powerful relationship with Him. And I would have been more useful.

Deceit is hypocrisy, and a hypocrite is someone who is acting out a role. It's the idea that you're playing the part of a nice, spiritual Christian at church or around other believers when, in reality, you are anything but that. The way to avoid this fatal flaw is to live the godly life at all times.

The Fatal Flaw of Sexual Immorality. Samson could have been one of the truly great men of God in the Bible, but he had a fatal flaw that Satan used to bring him down. Even though he had everything going for him and did a lot of great things, big strong Samson ended up blind, naked, powerless and the laughing stock of his enemies. Then he ended up dead. Samson's fatal flaw was sexual immorality. Judges 16:1 tells us that Samson went to Gaza one day and got caught in the snare of a prostitute. Everything went crashing downhill from there. He got sifted.

God wants us to be sexually pure in mind and body. First Thessalonians 4:3 is perfectly clear about it: "This is the will of God, your sanctification: that you should abstain from sexual immorality." Yet one of Satan's greatest traps today is the lure of lust and sexual immorality. Take pornography, for example. It's everywhere! It's so available – books, magazines, DVDs, TV, the Internet! Think about it: pornography of every conceivable type is only a few keystrokes away on your fifth grader's laptop. I've talked to many men who got hooked on Internet pornography in the privacy of their own home or office or hotel room. They were innocently surfing the Net, checking the news or sports, and stumbled onto a link that reeled them in. They wound up addicted. The stuff just dominated them. And nobody else knew about it. They were in the process of being sifted.

Husbands, you cannot love your wife the way Christ loved the church if you are addicted to lust, pornography and sexual immorality. There's just no way! Wives, there's no way you can love and honor your husband in purity if you are addicted to steamy romance novels and TV shows that celebrate extramarital affairs. Students and singles, there's no way you can avoid the fatal flaw of sexual immorality if you fill your mind with movies, music, magazines and websites that promote casual sex and ridicule abstinence before marriage.

You need to know where this barrage of impure media is coming from. It's not God's people who are writing the vulgar scripts and filling books and magazines and websites with provocative photos and articles. The church isn't producing the movies and TV shows. *The author of all this stuff is the enemy!* He intends to snag your mind and imagination and turn them away from the life of purity God desires. He wants to drag you down into his sewer of sexual impurity to ruin God's good plans for you. He wants to devour you.

Disarming the Devil's Schemes

What can we do about these fatal flaws? Here are six things that will help you disarm the enemy's schemes to bring you down.

1. Get your flaws out in the open. Address whatever flaw Satan is trying to exploit in your life and face it openly. There is something powerful about saying out loud, "I've got a problem in this area of my life." It brings the flaw out of the dark and into the light so you can deal with it. That's one of the secrets of success for Alcoholics Anonymous. An alcoholic never gets any help until he admits to a group of recovering alcoholics, "My name is _____ and I'm an alcoholic."

Opening up about your weakness to a pastor or counselor or group of praying Christian friends is important and powerful. But even more important is getting on your knees and confessing your sin before God who will forgive you, cleanse you and empower you to change into the person He wants you to be. Confessing your flaw and bringing it into the light is the first step to take in dealing with it.

2. Develop a tough attitude toward your flaws. When you allow the enemy to drag you into an area of weakness, you're playing with fire. You've got to get tough with it! You have to separate yourself from anything or anyone Satan may be using to snare you. If going to the Home Show every year causes you to covet things for your house that you can't afford, stay away from the Home Show. If some of the programs on TV fire up lustful thoughts, don't watch them. If you can't stop watching them, block them or unsubscribe to the channels that broadcast them – or get rid of your TV! If your busy life keeps you from spending time with Jesus in prayer and Bible study, start scratching things off your calendar. If your computer is getting you into trouble, maybe it's not worth owning one. For sure you need to install filters that block undesirable pop-ups and websites from appearing on your screen. If a friend at school is a bad influence on you, make the hard call and find a new friend.

3. Face your flaws in the power of the Holy Spirit. Do you realize that the same power that created the universe and the planet we live on dwells within you in the person of the Holy Spirit (Romans 8:9-11)? Do you realize that He is there to give you victory over the flaws that can pull you away from His plans for your life? It's true! Paul wrote, "Walk in the Spirit, and you shall not fulfill the lust of the flesh" (Galatians 5:16). That's why he commanded us, "Be filled with the Spirit" (Ephesians 5:18). Do you know what the word "filled" means in that verse? It means to be so *dominated* and *controlled by* the Spirit of the living Christ that there is no room in your life for any of this other junk. It's like filling a glass of water so full that if you try to add just one more drop, it will spill over. That's how the Spirit of God is to dominate our lives and leave no room for pride, independence, deceit and other flaws.

4. Starve your flaws to death. Let's say you decide to get serious about going on a diet. You want to cut out sweets and eat the right things. How successful will you be if you keep your freezer stocked with your favorite brand of ice cream?

Talk about not smart! You know if that ice cream is there, you're going to fall off the wagon and dig into it. The only way to stay away from tempting food is to keep it out of the house.

It's like that in the spiritual world. Romans 13:14 says, "Put on the Lord Jesus Christ, and make no provision for the flesh to fulfill its lusts." In order to starve out the flaws that draw you away from Christ, you may have to cut some things out of your life. Jesus said, "If your right eye causes you to sin, pluck it out and cast it from you…And if your right hand causes you to sin, cut it off and cast it from you" (Matthew 5:29-30). Now, He isn't talking about literally cutting off body parts and maiming yourself. But He is saying you might have to do something drastic, even if it means ending some relationships or getting rid of some possessions that are too tempting to keep around.

As soon as a wrong idea or image hits your mind, immediately reject it – throw it out – because your every thought and deed are under lock and key in obedience to Christ. And you've thrown away the key!

The battle starts in the mind, in your thought life. Paul urges us to bring "every thought into captivity to the obedience of Christ" (2 Corinthians 10:5). That's where your "starvation diet" must begin. As soon as a wrong idea or image hits your mind, immediately reject it – throw it out – because your every thought and deed are under lock and key in obedience to Christ. And you've thrown away the key!

5. Build relationships for accountability. One thing I've discovered about myself is that I'm not really serious about dealing with a problem until I do two things. First, I confess it to Jesus Christ and see it the way He sees it. Second, I sit down with another man eyeball to eyeball and say, "Hey, I've got a problem area in my life." Once a brother in Christ knows what I'm dealing with, he's going to pray with me and for me. He's also going to hold me accountable. He's going to stick a finger in my face from time to time and say, "How's it going in that area?" I know the areas where I'm gifted and strong. But I need somebody to hold my feet to the fire in areas where I'm not so strong.

In 2 Samuel 12, the prophet Nathan held King David accountable for adultery and murder with the convicting words "You are the man!" (v.7). You know what? If David had had a Nathan in his life long before then, maybe he wouldn't have gotten in trouble in the first place. He needed an accountability partner who knew him well enough to stick a finger in his face and say, "Don't go on that roof and fire up your lust for Bathsheba, David. It's going to be a disaster." But David didn't confess his flaws to anyone, and his sin brought him down.

This is why I encourage every man, every woman and every teen to have somebody in their life they can confess their problem areas to. Get a person who will listen to you, pray for you and check in with you about the issues you struggle with.

6. *Get professional help.* Some people have been holding onto baggage from their fatal flaws so long that they can't let go of it. If you're in that category, you may need more than a friend praying for you and holding you accountable. It may be time to seek out a godly professional counselor or pastor to help you identify the root causes of your problems and find victory.

What's the payoff from the hard work of battling your enemy and dealing with fatal flaws? For me, it's being able to finish strong for Jesus instead of ending up a casualty of Satan. I pray that I can look up to Jesus on my deathbed and say, "By your grace, I've honored You the best I could." And I want to be able to look at my wife and say, "I've been faithful to you all these years. There's been no other woman in my life." I want my kids to know that their dad may not have done everything perfectly, but – bottom line – he loved Jesus and experienced victory over the fatal flaws in his life. That's a payoff worth sacrificing for.

Winning the battle for your best is not just about eliminating flaws and sin in your life. This battle also has a positive side. In the next chapter, we'll talk about ways you can be proactive in replacing the wrong things in your life with the right things.

13

It's Never Wrong to Do the Right Thing

You've probably heard of Al Capone, the notorious Chicago mobster of the 1920s and 30s. But do you know about the man nicknamed "Easy Eddie" who was Capone's business partner in crime? Easy Eddie was a rich, successful lawyer and businessman before he moved to Chicago, who got even richer helping run Capone's crime syndicate.

One day Eddie had a change of heart. He volunteered to become a secret informant to the government, and his testimony helped put Al Capone in prison. Nobody knows for sure what caused Eddie to go straight. Some think he was just tired of working with thugs. Others say he wanted to avoid being arrested and sent to prison. And some believe Eddie decided to straighten up and try to be a better example for his only son who was his pride and joy. Whatever his reasons were, Eddie stepped up and did the right thing. Several years later he paid a great price for his good deed. He was gunned down in a gangland-style execution. He did the right thing and it cost him his life.

Here's another true example of doing the right thing. Lt. Commander E.H. "Butch" O'Hare was a decorated naval hero in World War II. One day

Butch O'Hare and five other fighter pilots took off from the U.S.S. Lexington to protect the carrier from approaching Japanese bombers. When Butch and his wingman spotted enemy planes, the other members of their squad were out of range. Even though they were outnumbered nine to two, Butch and his partner had to start the attack alone.

Right away the wingman's guns jammed, shrinking the odds to nine against one. Nobody would have blamed Butch for calling off the attack until the other fighters arrived. But if they didn't attack right away, some of the bombers might get through to the Lexington. Butch decided to take on all nine enemy planes alone, knowing he would be a sitting duck for the bombers' gunners. By the time the other fighter planes arrived, Butch O'Hare had shot down five enemy bombers and damaged a sixth. His heroic effort has been called one of the most daring achievements in the history of combat aviation. Butch was awarded the Medal of Honor for doing the right thing in the face of deadly odds.

Less than two years later, Lt. Commander O'Hare was shot down and perished during combat over the South Pacific. O'Hare International Airport was named in tribute to Edward H. "Butch" O'Hare in the same city – Chicago, Illinois – where Butch's dad, Edward J. "Easy Eddie" O'Hare paid the ultimate price to bring down Al Capone. We'll never know for sure, but I suspect that Butch O'Hare's heroics may have been inspired by his father's decision to do the "right thing."

Here's what I want to emphasize: *It doesn't matter what your dreams or calling from God may be – it won't come easy. You will have to battle for God's best in your life. And a big part of that battle will be "doing the right thing" consistently against all odds.* Mark Twain wrote, "Do the right thing. It will gratify some people and astonish the rest." I want to give you four reasons why doing the right thing every time is always the right thing to do.

Right Is Always Right

I heard a motto that goes something like this: "It is always right to do right, and it is always wrong to do wrong. It is never right to do wrong, and it is never wrong to do right." Now when I try to say that one out loud, it's a real tongue-twister; but it's packed with a lot of truth. The challenge for us is always to do the right thing because it is always right, regardless of the consequences. It's always the right thing no matter what anyone else is doing. It's always the right thing even though today many people believe there is no such thing as absolute right and wrong. We are called to do the right thing for no other reason than it is the right thing to do.

We have a big mess in our world today because too many people think it's OK to do the wrong thing. People find ways to justify their wrong actions, rationalize them as being right, or explain them away. For example, look at the whole drug and steroid scandal in college and professional sports. Consider the number of people in government who get caught in extramarital affairs or bribes or squandering taxpayers' money for personal benefit. When all the details come to light, they often say things like, "I'm so sorry. I was wrong." But before they are caught in the act, they keep living as if their wrongdoing is all right. For them the only time to do right is after they get busted for doing wrong.

The question is usually not what the right thing is but whether or not we are willing to do the right thing.

In every situation you face, the right thing to do is almost always plain to see. It's the honest thing, the truthful thing, the loving thing, the gracious thing, and the positive thing. The question is usually not what the right thing is, but whether or not we are willing to *do* the right thing.

I heard a story about a racquetball player who was competing in his first professional tournament. His opponent was a highly ranked champion in the sport. At match point in the fifth and deciding game the young rookie made a great shot off the wall to score the winning point. The referee and a linesman saw the shot and called it good. But the young man knew that his shot grazed the floor before it hit the wall, disqualifying the winning point. At that moment he had a decision to make: keep quiet and enjoy his first professional victory or tell the officials and let the game continue.

Well, this player did the right thing. He insisted to the officials that his shot wasn't good. His opponent took the serve and went on to win the match. Everyone was stunned. Here was a player who had victory in the bag but made a choice based on conviction and wound up losing the match. Why did he do it? The player later said something like, "I had to do it to maintain my integrity." This young man went on to become one of the greatest professional racquetball players to ever play the game.

This is our challenge every time we are faced with a choice. Am I going to do the right thing simply because it's the right thing? The right thing to do is always right wherever you are. Right is always right in your school classroom when someone offers you the answers to tomorrow's quiz and you know you will never get caught. You know what's right. Will you do the right thing? Right is always right when someone in your coffee group or supper club starts badmouthing the pastor or his wife. You know the right thing. Will you do the right thing? Right is always right in the workplace when you overhear your bosses plotting to fire an employee on false charges. You know the right thing to do. Will you do what is right?

F.B. Meyer said, "Do right because it is right to do right, then when you're misunderstood, ill-treated, when you're the victim of unjust suffering, you won't swerve, you won't sit down, you won't whine, you won't despair." If you are faithful to live the truth, speak the truth, and consistently do the right thing just because it's the right thing, you will never have to worry about being fake, phony or artificial. You won't have to keep looking over your shoulder, afraid of being caught, found out or exposed as a cheat. You can live every day with a clear conscience because you have left nothing in the closet that could someday jump out and accuse you.

Doing Right Is Always a Big Deal

According to a recent study reported in the *Washington Post*, one out of every one hundred adults in the United States is in prison. That's over 2.3 million adults locked up. The U.S. leads the world both in the number and percentage of its population behind bars.[2]

Do you know how all these men and women ended up in prison? In the vast majority of cases it started out with something small. Maybe as a child or teen they stole a candy bar or swiped a quarter from mom's purse or bullied a kid in school or chose to hang out with the wrong crowd or took a "tiny puff" from a joint or watched an x-rated video. It was the wrong thing to do and they knew it – but they did it anyway. Small things led to bigger things that led to bigger things that eventually led to prison.

Why did they step over the line to begin with? They did it by thinking the same way we often think about little things: It's just no big deal! They rationalized their actions by saying, "It's only a quarter and she'll never miss it" or "Just one puff won't make anybody a drug addict" or "Nobody will even notice" or "It's not hurting anybody." But when people step over the line in small things, the door opens a little wider for stepping over the line in bigger things. It's a slippery slope that can lead to blowing it in a huge way, costing you everything.

Jesus expressed the principle this way: "He who is faithful in what is least is faithful also in much; and he who is unjust in what is least is unjust also in much" (Luke 16:10). This is a principle for living. Do what is right in the little things, and you will do what is right in the big things. But if you fail to do what is right in the little things, you will also fail to do what is right in the big things. No matter how small the situation, if there is a right and wrong side, choose what is right. It may not be a life-changing issue, but by making the right choice in the little things, you are equipping yourself to make the right choice the next time when the stakes may be much higher.

Do Right Even If You're the Only One

One day during her junior high school years, a young friend of ours – whom I will call Lauren – learned an important lesson. Lauren and another friend had the same English teacher, but during two different periods. When Lauren went to school that morning, her friend said to her, "I didn't finish my

---

2 N.C. Aizenman, "New High in U.S. Prison Numbers," *Washington Post*, February 29, 2008, p.A01.

English homework. Let me copy your paper to turn in during my second period class, then at lunch I'll give the paper back to you to turn in during seventh period." So Lauren handed over her paper. She later said to our daughter Natalie, "I knew it was wrong but what could I do? She's my friend and asked for my help."

Well, Lauren couldn't find her friend at lunch to get her paper back, so she walked into seventh period English in a panic without the paper she was supposed to turn in. Suddenly her friend came into class, walked over to Lauren and handed her the paper. The teacher saw the whole thing, asked a few questions, and decided that the girls had cheated. She sent them both to the principal's office on the spot.

That evening after Natalie shared her friend's experience with me, I decided to use it as a teaching point with the whole family. I gave the kids a pep talk about doing the right thing for no other reason than it's just the right thing to do. Natalie responded, "Dad, I know it wasn't right, but everybody at school does it!" At that moment I launched into a profoundly inspired and eloquent discourse on the topic of doing the right thing even if you're the only one doing the right thing! The more I talked and waxed eloquently, the more I realized that this was a lesson for me and not just for my kids. How important it is, mom and dad, to always be truthful and fair in what we say and do. Young eyes are watching us. Waxing eloquently is meaningless unless we are walking honestly.

I'm afraid that the younger generation thinks it's all right to do the wrong thing today because the previous generation modeled that behavior for them.

We have a whole generation today that believes it's OK to do the wrong thing because other people are doing it. If you're a student, you know that cheating on homework and exams goes on all the time – and a bunch of kids get away with it. You know kids who text in class even though the rules forbid it. I'm afraid that the younger generation thinks it's all right to do the wrong thing today because the previous generation modeled that behavior for them.

It's tough to stand out in a crowd by doing the right thing when everybody else is doing the wrong thing. But right is right no matter how many people agree. In Luke 17, Jesus met ten lepers who cried out to Him for healing. Jesus said, "Go show yourselves to the priests" (v.14). In those days lepers were banished to leper colonies so they wouldn't infect others in the community. So a leper who was healed had to get the OK of the priests before he could return to the community. As these ten were on their way to the priests, they discovered that they were completely healed.

Everybody knows that when someone gives you a gift, the right thing to do is to express your thanks. It's a no-brainer. So one of the healed lepers turned around and headed back to thank Jesus. The other nine just kept going. I imagine that the tenth guy had a moment of indecision. "It's wrong not to thank the Master for healing me. But I feel a little weird doing the right thing all by myself." It took guts to go against the tide, but this man did it. He returned to Jesus and worshiped Him.

Then Jesus said, "Were there not ten cleansed? But where are the nine?" (v.17). In other words, "Your friends should be here, too. But you did the right thing." You may feel conspicuous doing what you know is right when everybody else is doing wrong, but we're not out to please the crowd. We're out to please God.

Do the Right Thing Even When It Costs You

According to one record of early church history, Telemachus was an eastern monk in the fourth century who made a pilgrimage to Rome. While there he came upon a stadium where gladiators were killing each other in front of a cheering crowd. The monk knew that such "sport" was abominable and wrong, so he determined to do something about it. He stepped out onto the field of combat and begged the gladiators to stop the slaughter. The spectators became so enraged that the games were being interrupted that they stoned Telemachus to death.

The monk's choice to do the right thing cost him his life, but his effort was not in vain. When the Roman Emperor heard about the monk's death, he put an end to the spectacle of organized gladiator combat in Rome – for good.

At times, doing the right thing will cost you dearly. Your stand probably won't cost as much as Telemachus's cost him, but it could cost you some serious discomfort, time, money or popularity. That's right, you may not be popular with everyone and you could lose a friend or two. But like the brave monk, if you are committed to doing the right thing every time – no matter what – who knows how much good will result from it?

Make the Right Choice

Here are four quick steps to help you develop a pattern of doing what is right.

1. Decide up front to do the right thing every time. This is a lifetime commitment. It's kind of like a marriage vow. You make the choice *now* so you don't have to think about it later on in the pressure of the moment. You say, "I will do the right thing – period!" That decision has been made once and for all.

2. Discover the right thing. In most situations the right thing to do will be obvious. But when it isn't, you need to discover it so you can do it. Think about it, pray about it, and seek input from others.

3. Determine to follow through. As soon as you know what to do, act on it. Don't put it off or try to talk yourself out of it. Pay the price and take the step. I like what President Woodrow Wilson said: "Tell me what is right and I will fight for it!"

4. Discipline your life according to what is right. The more consistently you do what is right, the more it will become second nature to you. It almost becomes an automatic response. I know of a dad and mom who have a small wooden paddle for those times when their children need to be "encouraged" to change wrong behavior to right behavior. They have a name for the paddle: Mr. Do Right. It works great for disciplining kids. But as a teen or an adult, you need to *be* your own Mr. Do Right to build into your life the "right" response every time.

Do you know what happens when you become a person who does the right thing every time no matter what? You can be proud of who you are. You can be proud of what you have achieved and what you've got. And you can be proud of how you got it. You can lay your head on the pillow at night and rest without shame because you did the right thing. You can relax without fear, knowing that nobody will show up at your door and take away your stuff because you got it the wrong way. When you do right because it is right in little things and big things, even if you are the only one doing the right thing, even if it costs you something – the end result is that you will be right for doing right.

How do you survive the ongoing battle for God's best in your life? You must have a power that gets you through all the negatives and enemies in your path, a power that fuels your drive to achieve your dreams and goals. Section V is about one key source of power you must have.

V

SOMEONE WHO BELIEVES

How to View and Value the Power of Belief

Now faith is the substance of things hoped for,
the evidence of things not seen.

HEBREWS 11:1

Faith is to believe what we do not see;
and the reward of this faith is to see what we believe.

ST. AUGUSTINE

14

I Believe

During the 1971 season, my freshman year at Baylor, our football team finished with a record of one win and ten losses. At the end of the season, the university hired a new head coach, Grant Teaff. He walked onto the campus and into our locker room with a whole new perspective. Coach Teaff is an example of what happens when someone shows up who believes some things and knows how to get things done. The first game of our 1972 season illustrates what I mean. The game against the University of Georgia Bulldogs in Athens, Georgia, was Coach Teaff's first game as our head coach and my first as the starting quarterback. Baylor had won only three games the previous three years and Georgia's "Dawgs" were picked by some experts to win the National Championship that year. Needless to say, they were good.

It was a blazing hot day, 113 degrees on the turf. When we took the field for warm-ups, 60,000 Georgia fans went crazy, screaming and chanting at us, "Dog meat! Dog meat! Dog meat!" Well, most of our guys were young, inexperienced and easily intimidated – including me. When we left the field after warm-ups, we were overwhelmed by the rabid fans and the prospects of going head to head with a nationally ranked team on their home turf.

Back in the locker room, Coach Teaff seized the moment and gave us a pep talk. I remember being fired up and inspired by what he said. It was a classic example of what a coach who really believes in himself and his system does when his players are down. He said, "Today I want you to play with pride, win or lose. I want you to walk out onto that field with pride. After the game I want you to walk off that field with pride, knowing that you gave your very best." And when Coach said "walk," that's exactly what he meant. He wanted us to walk onto the field in order to save energy in the oppressive heat. But he also wanted us to walk to show our pride – up on our cleats, heads high, shoulders back, looking the Georgia players square in the eye. And that's what we did. In fact, walking onto the field every game became our trademark for the rest of my career at Baylor, including our final game as champions in the Cotton Bowl on January 1, 1975.

We went out and played very well against Georgia. In fact, we might have had a chance to win if our starting quarterback hadn't thrown an interception late in the game as we were driving for a go-ahead touchdown. Yes, that was me. But our team did play with pride and fought to the end, losing by only ten points to the powerful Bulldogs. What made the difference? What happened to us between being intimidated out of our socks during warm-ups and giving the Georgia Bulldogs a good scare with our inspired effort? One thing: A man who believed *showed up!*

When someone shows up who truly believes, the power of belief makes things happen and changes things for the better.

When someone shows up who truly believes, the power of belief makes things happen and changes things for the better. It's just a powerful thing when someone who believes shows up. The husband or wife who *believes* can change a marriage. The child or teen who *believes* can change a whole school. A coach who *believes* can change a team. A mom who *believes* can change a home. A boss or employee who *believes* can change a company. A minister or lay leader who *believes* can change a congregation.

The power of belief turns losers into winners. In sports, for example, a poor team one year can go from "worst to first" to win a championship the next year when someone who believes shows up. Mediocre students who are inspired to belief and confidence by their teachers can become top students. A poorly producing division in the company can turn around and become the number one division in the region or the nation. How do things like this happen? There are a lot of factors involved, of course, but at the heart of a powerful turnaround or great victory there is usually someone bold enough to believe that things can change for the better.

The power of belief is indispensible for getting you through the trials and troubles that stand between you and God's best for your life. This chapter is all about inspiring the power of belief in your soul so that you will be a powerful influence for change wherever and whenever *you* show up.

Belief that Changes Things

What you believe defines who you are, reveals what you value, shapes how you live, and determines your success. I'm talking about your beliefs about yourself, about others, about life, about today and tomorrow, about handicaps and defeats, about dreams and setbacks, about eternity, about God, about everything. What you believe will impact how you go through life and what you will do with whatever life throws at you. Most people tend to go through life with doubt instead of belief. They think "I can't" or "I'm not that smart" or "I'm not good enough" or "I'm not gifted." They need someone who believes in them before they can believe in themselves. They need to hear others say "You can do it," "You can learn," and "You can become what you want to be." There is great power in parents, teachers, coaches, ministers and others who believe and ignite belief in others.

The kind of belief I'm talking about is tied to something specific. It has an object. Saying "I believe" doesn't mean much unless there is something "great" you believe *in*. Do you know what is amazing about what you believe in? It doesn't have to be something you can fully understand, explain, or even defend for it to be powerful or make a difference in your life. For example, one of the things I choose to believe in is Baylor University football. I mean, cut me and I bleed Baylor green and gold. Now, some people think I'm stupid to believe in a football program. I'm not smart enough to give you an ironclad argument for believing in Baylor, but let me tell you more about the transformations that occurred in Baylor football as a result of one man's belief.

Coach Teaff's theme for the 1972 season was "pride" – *Play with pride and restore pride in Baylor University football.* After the loss at Georgia we went on to win five of our remaining ten games, nearly doubling our total wins over the past three seasons. Even though we had a losing record of 5-6, Coach Teaff was named "Coach of the Year" in the Southwest Conference for inspiring such an incredible turnaround.

The 1973 season for Coach Teaff and Baylor football was a tough one. We played pretty well at times but lost several close games and finished the season with only two wins – 2-9. At the close of the season it seemed like everybody was down on Baylor football. Students, fans, alumni and the media were ragging on us. Baylor can't win. Baylor can't compete with football powers like Texas and Arkansas. But Coach Teaff believed! He believed in himself, he believed in us, and he believed that Baylor football could be competitive. I vividly remember sitting in a team meeting at the end of that disappointing 2-9 season. Coach made this statement: "You are a loser only if you believe you are a loser. No one will ever convince me that I'm a loser or that you're a loser or that this football team is a loser." Those powerful words stuck with me all through the off season.

In a team meeting the following spring, Coach Teaff announced our theme for the 1974 season: I BELIEVE. Now when he unveiled that motto, there weren't many people anywhere who believed in us or believed that '74 would be any better than '73. But Coach Teaff believed in himself, in us, and in our team, and his belief powerfully impacted every player on that team. "It doesn't matter what anybody else believes about our team," Coach would say. "The only thing that matters is what *you* believe about our team. Do *you* believe?"

Well, we started to believe. In 1974, Baylor went from last place to first place in the Southwest Conference. We turned around the previous year's 0-7 conference record to 6-1. Our overall record improved from 2-9 in '73 to 8-3 in '74. And at the end of the season we were no longer conference doormats but conference champions. Of course, by then everyone was jumping on the bandwagon. Everyone believed in Baylor! But it didn't matter to our team if anyone else believed in us or not. We had answered Coach Teaff's question, "Do you believe in this team?" with an enthusiastic "Yes!" What mattered was that *we* believed and the power of that belief dramatically impacted our football team and what happened on the field. The whole football program changed when Coach Teaff – a man who believed – showed up!

Do You Believe?

I'll ask you the same question Coach Teaff asked us: Do you believe? I'm not asking if you believe in Baylor football. I'm asking if you believe in God. I'm asking if you believe in yourself as a person of high value because you have been created and gifted by God. I'm asking if you believe in your dreams and calling from God. I'm asking if you believe in your family and your church. When I say *believe*, I'm not talking about a wimpy emotion that hopes something will happen or wishes somebody would do something. Martin Luther said, "Faith is a living, daring confidence in God's grace, so sure and certain that a man could stake his life on it a thousand times." The kind of belief that transforms people and situations is the confidence that something will happen as I focus on who I am and what God has called me to do.

What I'm getting at is this: *If you believe, positive things will happen wherever and whenever you show up. So believe!* If you're a student, what would happen if you showed up at school with a daring confidence that God was going to use you to demonstrate His power and love through the way you live? You could help change the spiritual climate of your school. As an employee, when you decide to show up at work with a strong, positive belief in the value of your company and clients, you could help improve morale among the staff and maybe even shore up the bottom line. As a spouse, parent, or child, you would be blown away by the transformation in your family if you decide to show up with a bold belief in the value of every family member and a commitment to serve each other in love.

Charles Kettering, who invented the electric starter for cars, summarized his secret of success this way: "Believe and act as if it is impossible to fail." A person with unswerving conviction and belief in God, a person who is willing to stand up for his or her values and share something that impacts others in a positive way is a powerful force. A person like that can change a situation and the views of others in that situation.

I strongly believe that how people live is the direct result of how big they believe their God is. The problem is that many people don't know God, or their view of God is too small. They are not convinced that they are absolutely safe, because they don't see God as fully competent, all-knowing and ever-present. When you live with a small God, you wake up every morning fearful and anxious because so much depends on you. Your whole mood will be governed by your circumstances and your ability to manage them.

When people with a small God have a chance to share their faith or do anything that stretches their abilities, they shrink in fear because they don't think God will come through for them. They can't handle the rejection or ridicule. If they don't live in the security of a big God's acceptance, they become slaves to what others think of them. If you shrink God from what He really is, you will pray without faith, work without passion, serve without joy and suffer without hope. The result is fear, retreat, loss of vision and failure to persevere. In order to experience the power of belief, you must be convinced that this earth is in the hands of an infinite God whose character and competence can be fully trusted. It's the only way you can pray along with authors Bill and Kathy Peel, "Lord, help me do great things as though they were little, since I do them with Your power; and little things as though they were great, since I do them in Your name."[3]

> *If you shrink God from what He really is, you will pray without faith, work without passion, serve without joy and suffer without hope.*

---
3 Bill and Kathy Peel, *Discover Your Destiny* (Colorado Springs, CO: NavPress, 1997), p.215.

Transforming Faith in God

Almost everybody has heard the great Bible story of David and Goliath. It's a prime example of what can happen when someone like a young shepherd boy named David shows up with belief in a big God. Here's the scene from 1 Samuel 17. King Saul and the army of Israel are on one side of the valley Elah and the army of the Philistines is on the other side. The Philistines' main guy is Goliath, a giant warrior described to be around nine feet tall. He challenged Israel to send out one of their warriors to fight him one on one.

Well, everybody in Israel was terrified of Goliath, and nobody wanted to take on this giant. The Israelites were intimidated and overwhelmed – just like my teammates and me before the Georgia game. But then somebody who believed showed up! This believer wasn't a buffed-out, muscle-bound gladiator like Goliath. He wasn't even an experienced soldier from the army of Israel. He was a keeper of sheep who was probably in his teens at the time. David wasn't equipped with state-of-the-art weapons and armor. All he had was a little slingshot and a big belief in God that changed everything.

When David saw Goliath, he saw the same nine-foot ogre the Israelites saw. But instead of looking for someplace to hide, he said "[I] will go fight with this Philistine" (1 Sam. 17:32). What was the difference? All King Saul and his army could see was how big Goliath was. All David could see was how big God was and what He could do. And he believed in God. He said confidently, "The Lord…will deliver me from the hand of this Philistine" (v.37). And we all know what happened.

I choose to believe in the God of the Bible and in Jesus Christ his Son as my Lord and Savior. Some people think I'm as crazy to believe in Jesus as I am to believe in Baylor football. They say there's no reason to believe in Him. Some laugh at me, some think I'm naïve, and some say I am misguided. But I believe in Jesus, and the power of that belief has changed my life! It doesn't matter what anyone says about what I believe. My belief in God has changed everything!

My belief in God and Jesus is my *choice*. I *choose* to believe. Even though I can't fully explain it, I choose to believe even when I can't understand why things go wrong or get difficult. I choose to say along with the ninth-century theologian Anselm of Canterbury, "I do not seek to understand in order to believe, but I believe in order to understand."

What do you do when your child contracts a rare bone disease in his knees? This is what happened to our son James as a teenager. He suffered through three major surgeries, two on his right knee and one on his left. He was on crutches for eleven months that year. I hated the haunting sound of those crutches on the floor as James hobbled around the house because I knew what he was having to go through. The doctors couldn't promise us that he would even walk again, much less play sports. How do you maintain belief in a powerful, loving God when something like that happens? Well, you keep on believing in a good God even when bad things start happening. I questioned God at times. James and I had several heart-to-heart talks about what was happening to him. He would say through his tears, "Why me, Dad? Why is this happening to me?" I didn't have a pat answer, and I knew I couldn't bluff him with old clichés. So I said, "James, there are a lot of things I don't know, so I'm not going to major on what I *don't* know. I'm going to major on what I *do* know. What I do know is that God is good, and He is going to use this problem with your knees to accomplish something good in your life and to bring about His purposes for His glory." Our faith had to show up.

What do you do when your wife is told she has breast cancer, as my wife Sheila was? You may know from personal experience what it feels like to hear that your wife or mother or daughter needs a mastectomy and that the chances of a complete recovery may not be good – that the cancer might be terminal. You may know what it's like to be with her just before surgery. She's on the hospital bed, you pray with her and kiss her, and then they roll her through those doors for the surgery. You begin to have thoughts like I did: *What am I going to do? Is this the beginning of the end of my wife's life and our life together?*

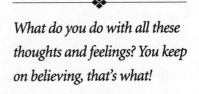

What do you do with all these thoughts and feelings? You keep on believing, that's what!

Am I soon to be a widower and a single father? Are my kids about to lose their mother? What do you do with all these thoughts and feelings? You keep on believing, that's what! I had to keep believing in a God who loves my wife more than I do, and loves me and my kids. And I had to believe that God was going to accomplish His perfect will in the situation. Somehow He would do something that would bring Him honor and glory and bless my family.

What do you do when you stand at the grave of a loved one – a parent, a spouse, a child? What do you do when your parents tell you they're going to split up? What do you do when your kids walk away from the faith into a destructive lifestyle? What do you do when the pink slip arrives on your desk and your wife is six months pregnant with twins? You may doubt, you may cry, you may get angry – but you keep on believing in God. You believe that He is sovereign, loving, all-powerful, and knows exactly what He's doing or allowing to happen. You believe that Jesus has conquered death and evil and will give eternal life to anyone who believes in Him as Savior and Lord. You may not feel like believing, but you *choose* to believe in a God who loves you and is working out His purposes for your good and His glory. You show up with faith.

Faith for a lot of people is attached to a big "if." They say, "*If* everything goes well for me, *if* no one in my family dies, *if* my parents let me do what I want, *if* my business grows, *if* I make the team – then I will believe." But real belief happens when we say "though" instead of "if." Real faith says, "*Though* I struggle, *though* I lose my investments, *though* I don't get everything I want, *though* I lose a loved one tragically – I still choose to believe." Faith is having confidence in God no matter what comes my way. We learn to say with Job, "Though He slay me, yet will I trust Him" (Job 13:15).

It's Better to Believe

Why is it so difficult to believe God in the midst of our pain and doubt? I think there are several negative thoughts we allow to siphon away our faith and belief in God.

I can't do it. This statement isn't even biblical. It's much better to say with

Paul, "I can do all things through Christ who strengthens me" (Philippians 4:13). Warren McVea was one of the best athletes to come out of the state of Texas. He played college and professional football in the 1960s and 70s and was the Texas state 100-meter champion at the University of Houston. The guy they called "Wondrous Warren" had a great can-do attitude. He used to tell the sprinter next to him at the start of a race, "Just hang onto me and I'll get you second place." I love it! The statement "I can't" is a belief killer. "I can" is a belief thriller! "I can" is biblical and ignites situation-changing belief.

> *The statement "I can't" is a belief killer. "I can" is a belief thriller! "I can" is biblical and ignites situation-changing belief.*

I've hit the ceiling. People camped on this negative thought assume they have gone as far as they can go. "I'm tapped out, maxed out and burned out," they say. But according to the Bible, there is no ceiling. Think about how many times in Scripture God says, "I will do a new thing." First Corinthians 2:9 says, "Eye has not seen, nor ear heard, nor have entered into the heart of man the things which God has prepared for those who love Him." And Paul isn't talking about the "sweet bye-and-bye" in this verse; this promise is for the "bitter here-and-now." There may be a thousand reasons why you can't get to the next level, but they're all lies. Nothing can hold you back unless you give it permission to hold you back. The sky's the limit for the person who believes.

It's too late for me – I am what I am. Some people argue, "You can't teach an old dog new tricks. You are what you are so you just have to live with it." Well, first of all, you're not an old dog. You're a person of infinite value created in the image of God. C.S. Lewis wrote, "We are what we believe we are." So it's best to believe that you are what God says you are: a brand new creation with unlimited promise and potential.

Second, the things God does when someone who believes shows up are not tricks. They are God's marvelous works in response to what you believe and how you act on your belief. It's never too late to change or start over. Anytime is a good time to change, and no time is better than right now – this moment

– today! Now is the time to *step up* and make a decision about what must be done, *step away* from everything that hinders you, and *step out* and just do it! Take that leap of faith!

I can't get there from here. You may think that believing in your big dreams and great potential is unrealistic because these things look impossible to reach from where you are now. The fact is that champions, leaders and significant achievers are usually never realistic about what they set out to do, but they believe they can do it anyway and then act on that belief. Crossing the ocean to find the New World was unrealistic until Christopher Columbus believed it could be done and accomplished the "impossible." Sending men to the moon was unrealistic until NASA engineers believed and made it happen. Sure, there are risks that come along with shooting for the stars in your life. You may fail a number of times before you succeed. But just because you struck out last time doesn't mean you will strike out the next time.

Good things don't happen to people like me. That's a big lie! Good things – even great things – happen to people like you all the time. Look at me, for example. What chance did a stuttering kid have to play football in the NFL and enjoy a fulfilling ministry as a preacher and speaker? Well, my chances were somewhere between zip and zero if I believed that it could never happen. But I kept moving in the direction of my beliefs and many of the good things I envisioned became reality. You may not achieve everything you want to achieve, but you won't achieve anything if you don't step up to the plate and step out on your beliefs. You've got to show up!

The word going around the valley of Elah that day was that Goliath was bigger, stronger, better trained, and more heavily armed than David, and that the giant would squash the puny little shepherd boy like a bug on a freeway. But God was on David's side, and He had the last word on this battle. God's word was, "I'm bigger and stronger than Goliath, I will win this battle for Israel, and the giant will fall dead in his tracks." The word on me was that becoming a preacher was impossible. That's what everybody thought, and it's even what I thought. But God always has the last word, and I choose to believe the word of the God who said He would use my life and even my stuttering to make a difference for His glory.

What's the word on you? What do people say is unrealistic or impossible for you to accomplish or become? Well, don't believe a word of it until you hear God's last word on the subject. Choose to believe what God says you can accomplish and become, because His word is what matters.

True belief is always a two-step process. First, you choose to believe, and second, you show up and act on that belief. In the next chapter, we will take that second step.

15

Make a Play

Dr. Evan O'Neil Kane was chief surgeon at Kane-Summit Hospital in New York City in the early 20th century. He was 60 years old and had been practicing surgery for 37 years. He was especially interested in the expanded use of *local* anesthesia. Back then, the primary anesthesia used for more serious cases was *general* in nature, and it had its complications. Patients were sometimes left paralyzed and occasionally even died. Dr. Kane wanted to prove that local anesthesia could be used successfully in more than just simple, topical cases, so he began looking for a willing volunteer for surgery to prove his point. It was not easy to find such a person, however, because of the fear that the anesthetic would wear off early or would not be adequate to begin with.

Finally, on Tuesday morning, February 15, 1921, a patient with an inflamed appendix was rolled into the operating room where Kane had performed hundreds of appendectomies. He made the initial incision, skillfully removed the appendix just like he had many times before, and closed up. Through it all, the patient experienced only minor discomfort, recuperated quickly and was released from the hospital two days later with no lingering side effects.

Dr. Kane achieved his objectives with the surgery: 1) to prove that a person could undergo *major* surgery – while still awake – and recover quickly; and 2) to further inspire patients' trust in surgeons.

What *really* inspired trust, however, was not simply that the local anesthesia worked, but that Dr. Kane – unable to find a willing volunteer – *had operated on himself.* That's right, with the help of mirrors, a couple of assistants, and a local anesthetic, Dr. Kane cut open his own abdomen, removed his inflamed appendix and sewed himself up. He could have argued for years trying to convince doctors and patients about his belief in the expanded use of local anesthesia. Instead, he *showed up* and put his belief into action. While others watched in skepticism from the sidelines, Dr. Evan O'Neil Kane stepped up and made a play.

This is a key point about belief: The power of your belief will impact others only when you demonstrate what you believe through your actions. I call it "making a play." Henry David Thoreau wrote, "Live your beliefs and you can turn the world around." Notice that he didn't say "believe and you can turn the world around." The power of your belief is unleashed by demonstrating your belief. James 2:20 says it this way: "Faith without works is dead." If you believe but don't make a play to demonstrate your belief,

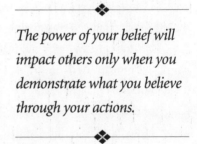

The power of your belief will impact others only when you demonstrate what you believe through your actions.

then your belief is dead, and there is no power in something that is dead.

In order to make a play, you have to be a person ready for action. You must be willing to take risks. You have to be in the game, not in the grandstand. You have to be on the front line of battle, not on R&R cooling your heels. You have to step out of your comfort zone into the risk zone and become involved instead of hanging back to see what everybody else is going to do. A person who makes a play is willing to pull out all the stops and take big risks to get a win.

Belief Is Demonstrated by Behavior

When the Israelites were facing Goliath and the Philistines, the whole situation changed because a shepherd boy who believed in a great God showed up. But David's great belief didn't end Goliath's threat until he made a bold play of faith with his slingshot. The Bible is full of examples of belief being demonstrated through action. Naaman demonstrated his belief by washing seven times in the river before he was cured of leprosy (2 Kings 5). By faith Gideon made a play by reducing his army to 300 so God could deliver Israel from the Midianites (Judges 6-7). Peter never walked on water until he made a play and stepped out of the boat, demonstrating his belief in Jesus (Matthew 14).

If you're going to experience a greater measure of God's power in your life, it will involve both believing and making a play that demonstrates how much you believe. You must begin by acting on your belief, which means trusting God enough to take steps of obedience and courage. Simply acknowledging information or giving mental assent to the truth is not enough. You have to get your feet wet. Here are a few suggestions that will put legs under your faith for making a play that can transform a situation.

Declare your belief. David said it in front of God and everybody: He would go fight Goliath, and God would help him bring down the giant. He wasn't naïve; he saw the reality of the situation. Goliath was big, powerful, and bad. But God was bigger, more powerful, and good. That's why David could make such a bold statement of belief. The first step in getting over the hurdles standing between you and God's plans for you is to declare what you believe about the situation and what you know God wants you to do.

Make a plan. In 1 Samuel 17:38-40, the king insisted that David go out to fight Goliath wearing the king's armor and sword. But David had to use a plan that was right for him, which included a sling, five stones and no body armor. This plan fit what he knew, what he had at hand, and what his experience, background and preparation called for. Advice from other people can be helpful at times, but we need to seek out God's plan for what He has called us to do.

Take a step. Move out by faith and take that first step. Belief doesn't stand around waiting for somebody else to make a move. It starts moving boldly in the direction of God's plan. The passage continues, "David hurried and ran toward the army to meet the Philistine" (v.48). Once you declare what God wants you to do and have His plan in mind, make a bold move and go for it!

Go in faith, not fear. The closer David got to Goliath, the bigger the giant looked. Here's a young guy who was probably around five and a half feet tall, and he's running head-on to take on a champion fighter who outmatched him in every way – nearly. You see, David had some help that day. So he ran fearlessly toward Goliath to get within range of his slingshot, knowing all the while that his God was bigger and stronger than Goliath.

The Israelites had fallen back in fear, focused on the situation, but David ran forward in faith – focused on the solution. The lesson for you and me is to keep our eyes on Jesus and do what He wants us to do.

> *The Israelites had fallen back in fear, focused on the situation, but David ran forward in faith – focused on the solution.*

Get the victory. David made a play based on his trust in God's plan and power, and he came out victorious. God showed up and performed a miracle through a shepherd boy. David and Israel gained the victory over the Philistines, and God got the glory. Everything changed for the whole nation of Israel when David showed up and made a play. Wars are won when soldiers make a play. Businesses succeed when employees make a play. Teams win when players make a play. Victories happen when someone who believes shows up and makes a play.

In his book *D-Day,* historian Stephen Ambrose tells the inspiring story of Lt. Robert Mathias, a platoon leader in the 82nd Airborne Division during the World War II invasion of Normandy. As the C-47 carrying Mathias and his paratroopers approached the drop site in the darkness, it began to take some flak from German guns on the ground. Then the red light flashed on over the open door of the plane signaling that it was time to get ready to jump.

Mathias ordered his sixteen men to stand and hook up their chute lines behind him. Then he stepped to the open door, ready to jump the moment the pilot flashed the green light. Suddenly a shell burst outside the plane and red-hot flak ripped into Mathias' chest, knocking him to the floor of the plane. Seriously wounded, he struggled to his feet and resumed his post at the door.

Then the green light flashed on. It was time to jump.

Lt. Mathias could have moved out of the way so the men behind him could jump. If he had done that, the crew of the C-47 might have patched up his wounds and gotten him back to England. Instead, Mathias yelled out, "Follow me!" and jumped into the night with his platoon right behind him. When Lt. Mathias was located on the ground about a half hour later, he was still in his chute, dead. He had made a courageous, self-sacrificing play and was the first American officer killed by German fire on D-Day. By believing strongly and making a play like Mathias did, his men advanced to the next level and helped win the war!

Here's how you win in life. You believe and then you make a play that demonstrates your belief. Whenever and wherever you show up to make a play in God's power, situations will change and God will be glorified. It happened with Moses and Israel facing the Red Sea. They believed in their God and His miracle-working power, but they had to make a play by stepping into the water before God opened a path for them on dry ground. It happened to Peter on the Sea of Galilee. All the disciples believed in Jesus' power, but only Peter made a play by climbing over the side of the boat and stepping out onto the water.

Whenever and wherever you show up to make a play in God's power, situations will change and God will be glorified.

Making a play in life is the same as making a play in sports or business or battle. If you believe in something deeply but don't make a play, you lose. The only way you can win is by demonstrating your belief, even if it costs you.

Making the Big Plays

There are times when you're called to make a very big play in a very important situation. These are opportunities where failing to make the play means losing out on something very special that God has for you. Here are a couple of them.

Demonstrating belief in Jesus Christ. Anyone who has seen a Billy Graham Crusade on television knows what Dr. Graham does at the end of each message. He invites people in the audience to receive Jesus Christ as their Savior. He leads them in a simple prayer they can pray silently right where they are sitting. Then he asks them to demonstrate their new belief by leaving their seats and coming forward to stand in front of the platform.

Romans 10:9 says, "If you confess with your mouth the Lord Jesus and believe in your heart that God has raised him from the dead, you will be saved." Belief is all about acknowledging in your heart that Jesus is the crucified and resurrected Son of God. Confession is demonstrating your belief. Your confession of faith may include going forward in church or simply telling someone, "I am a believer in Jesus Christ now." Your belief in Jesus was never meant to be a secret. Make the big play by acknowledging your belief in the presence of others.

Demonstrating belief through obedience. Another important way to demonstrate your belief in Jesus is to do what He says. We receive Jesus not just as Savior but also as Lord. This means He's the boss! Jesus said, "Why do you call Me, 'Lord, Lord,' and not do the things which I say?" (Luke 6:46). He's saying that you demonstrate your faith by handing over to Him the controls of your life. Believers don't tell God what to do; they ask God what He wants them to do – then they do it. If you don't make this play and continue to run your life your own way, you will miss everything that God has planned for you.

The Apostle Paul made this play the moment he was converted. When a light from heaven knocked him to the ground and Jesus spoke to him, Paul said, "Lord, what do you want me to do?" (Acts 9:6). And for the rest of his life, Paul demonstrated his belief in the Lord Jesus by doing everything the Lord told him to do.

Not everybody makes this play when they have the chance. Some people tell God they will do what He says, but when they find out what God wants, they won't do it. A young religious leader came to Jesus and asked what he must do to demonstrate his belief. He seemed to be very sincere in his faith because he had kept the commandments ever since he was a kid. Then Jesus said to him,

"Sell all that you have and distribute to the poor, and you will have treasure in heaven; and come, follow Me" (Luke 18:22). This was a major play that would dramatically change this guy's life. But because he was rich and didn't want to give everything away, he turned his back on Jesus.

There are a lot of people in church today like this rich young man. They have professed faith in Jesus as Savior so they can go to heaven. They may even have gone forward and been baptized. But they are not interested in doing what He says. They continue to set their own goals and live out their own plans without seriously asking God what He wants them to do. They're not making a play – they're play-acting – and they wind up missing out on God's best.

The power of belief is most clearly seen in people who demonstrate their faith by doing what God says – no matter what. I recently heard about a pastor from the eastern United States who had a successful, growing church for ten years. He had started the church from scratch, thousands of people had been reached, and lives were being changed every week. But one day God began saying that He wanted them to start a church from scratch on the Las Vegas strip that would reach out to the thousands of people who work in the hotels, casinos and clubs.

Well, this couple wasn't sure they wanted to raise their kids in a place some people say is located somewhere between Sodom and Gomorrah and hell! To them, God's direction seemed overwhelming, a little like being sent out to fight Goliath. But they had witnessed God's incredible power for ten years in a church that started from nothing and grew to thousands. As God's direction for them became clearer, they said "Yes, Lord" and made a play. The pastor and his family moved to Las Vegas and are now prayerfully working with a team getting ready to launch a brand new church right in the heart of "Sin City." How great is that!

Big plays are about Goliath-sized stuff, life-changing stuff. I'm talking about things like pulling up stakes and moving to Las Vegas if God tells you to. I'm talking about deciding on a career or changing careers or choosing the person you will marry or deciding to remain single. In these big things you have to find out what God wants you to do and then do it.

Your big-play choices will often appear between what seems logical and reasonable to you and what God is telling you to do, which may appear neither logical nor reasonable at the time. For example, David might have thought that retreating from a giant with a huge sword made a lot more sense than charging him with a slingshot. Yet the Bible teaches us, "Trust in the Lord with all your heart, and lean not on your own understanding" (Proverbs 3:5). God isn't against logic or reason. We simply must lean on His direction more than on our own understanding.

When a big, life-changing play comes up, seek God with all your heart, draw on the wisdom and insight He has given you, and you'll know what to do. Follow His leading, continue to seek His power and make the play! When God reveals His big play to you, it may be difficult and it may cost you something – even your life. Just think about all the Christians over the centuries and around the world who have been martyred just for confessing their belief in Jesus. Will you demonstrate your belief and make a big play no matter what it might cost?

Making the Little Plays

Really big situations that call for life-changing demonstrations of belief don't come along too often. They are like the handful of game-changing plays in a football game that end up on the highlight clips, such as a critical defensive play or a last-second field goal. But every day you face smaller, less significant opportunities, choices or decisions where you still have to make a play. In football, these are like the blocks and runs and catches that never make it to the highlight reel. But little plays made consistently are as important to victory as the big plays.

Proverbs 3:6 says, "In all your ways acknowledge Him, and He shall direct your paths." Notice that it says *all* your ways – every situation and opportunity that comes along in day-to-day life. If you want the Lord to keep you on the right path making the right plays, you need to acknowledge Him. The New Living Translation says, "Seek His will in all you do." The Bible makes the will of God clear in a lot of common, everyday areas of life so we can make small but important plays like these:

- Make a play by walking in purity in the midst of a world that is impure.
- Make a play by honoring your parents even though lots of kids don't honor theirs.
- Make a play by loving your spouse the way the Bible tells you to.
- Make a play by living with integrity and honesty so that your word is your bond.
- Make a play by telling others how awesome it is to know Jesus as your Savior.
- Make a play by being an example to your kids of the man or woman God wants them to be.

But what about those situations where God's direction for you isn't so obvious? There is an awesome little prayer in the Old Testament you can use on a day-by-day, moment-by-moment basis to seek God's will for making a play. The nation of Judah was about to be attacked by an enemy army. King Jehoshaphat had to make a play, but he didn't know what to do. So he "set himself to seek the Lord" (2 Chronicles 20:3), then he gathered the people together and prayed a great prayer ending with these words: "We do not know what to do, but our eyes are upon you" (v.12 NIV). God answered that prayer by showing Jehoshaphat and Judah exactly what to do, and a great victory occurred.

"Lord, I don't know what to do, but my eyes are on you." That's a powerful little prayer! It's kind of like a portable GPS, small enough to take with you anywhere. Need to know which road to take during a trip? Check the GPS with a few quick taps. Need guidance in a moment of indecision in your life? Don't just sit there waiting for something to happen. Say a quick prayer asking God for direction and then make a play based on how He leads you.

What do you do when you believe and make a play, but nothing happens? The next chapter answers that question.

16

I'm Still Here!

"Winners never quit and quitters never win." That familiar slogan was on a big sign in our high school locker room. The theme was drilled into our heads as athletes: Never give up! "Quit" was not in our vocabulary. The great General Douglas MacArthur said, "Age wrinkles the body. Quitting wrinkles the soul." No matter how impossible the odds, no matter how badly you may be losing the game, even if you are not playing well and everything seems to be going against you, you hang tough until you can turn it around. When the chips are down, you snap on your chin strap and stay in the game.

Do you know what makes champions in sports or any other area? Obviously, it helps to start with a degree of talent, but in order to rise to championship level, you need a deep resolve to keep going in tough times, stay the course when you are swamped by the storm, press on against all odds and obstacles, and, as Winston Churchill famously said, "Never, never, never, never give up!" Just like most athletes, I was taught from my earliest years as a competitor that the virtues of endurance, perseverance and tough-mindedness were the only path to victory and glory. Listen to what some champion athletes have said:

- *You become a champion by fighting one more round. When things are tough, you fight one more round.* James J. Corbett, heavyweight boxing champion

- *I never give up in a match. However down I am, I fight until the last ball.* Bjorn Borg, professional tennis champion
- *Ambition is the path to success. Persistence is the vehicle you arrive in.* Bill Bradley, former NBA basketball star and former U.S. Senator
- *Paralyze resistance with persistence.* Woody Hayes, college football coach
- *Gold medals aren't really made of gold. They're made of sweat, determination, and a hard-to-find alloy called guts.* Dan Gable, Olympic wrestling champion
- *The difference between the impossible and the possible lies in a man's determination.* Tommy Lasorda, professional baseball manager
- *I ran and ran and ran every day, and I acquired this sense of determination, this sense of spirit that I would never, never give up, no matter what happened.* Wilma Rudolph, Olympic track and field champion

The themes of perseverance and determination are vital to the power of your belief and to the impact of showing up to make a play. In Ephesians 6, the Apostle Paul describes our life as a spiritual battle "against principalities, against powers, against the rulers of the darkness of this age, against spiritual hosts of wickedness in the heavenly places" (v.12). This is bigger than playing a game; this is the lifelong struggle to victory against our enemy Satan. Paul encourages us to put on the whole armor of God to fight the battle. Then he closes with this powerful phrase: "Being watchful to the end with all perseverance" (v.18).

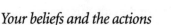

Your beliefs and the actions that demonstrate them will change a situation if you persevere and don't quit.

Here's my point: *You become a champion in life just as you become a champion in sports – by hanging tough when the going gets tough, by persevering to the very end, and by never giving up.* Your beliefs and the actions that demonstrate them will change a situation if you persevere and don't quit.

Going the Distance

I was deeply impacted by the power of perseverance at a critical point in my football career at Baylor. During the 1973 football season, my junior year, we finished with a dismal overall record of 2-9. Our last game was against Rice University, a pretty bad team that year. They beat us 27-0 and we ended up dead last in the Southwest Conference. It was one of the lowest moments of my entire life.

Coach Teaff called us together at the end of the Rice game and our disappointing season. He said he wanted us to begin our off-season conditioning program next week instead of waiting until after the Christmas and New Year holidays. Coach challenged each of us to search our hearts to see if we were committed to turning Baylor into a winning program. Anybody making that commitment was asked to show up Monday for off-season conditioning. Anybody unable to make that commitment could walk away right then and there, no questions asked.

All of us knew what this meant. Coach Teaff was challenging us to take our game to another level, to work harder and to sacrifice more. I'm sure the other guys had the same thought I had: *Do I really want to make this commitment, knowing all the time and pain and sacrifice that will be required?* And yet the whole team showed up on Monday to get a head start on next season. Well, our greatest fears were realized. It was a tough off-season, the most difficult, most strenuous workouts I have ever been through. Coach pushed us hard, demanding more from us and expecting us to give everything we had in every workout. As tough as the workouts were, when the days seemed darkest, something would happen to lift us up, encourage us and remind us why we were busting our tails.

It happened in the weight room where we spent hours pumping iron, stretching, and so on – repetition after repetition. It was so tough that at times I had thoughts of quitting, and I'm sure many of my teammates felt the same way. But during some of the hardest times, one of our young linebackers would stoke the fire in all of us when he would yell out in a booming voice three words: "I'm still here!" Because of all the fatigue and pain and agony, *phonetically* it sounded like some kind of desperate, groaning scream – "Ahm sti heah!" Every time he yelled those words he was reminding us, "Hey, I'm hurting as much as you are. This is as hard for me as it is for you. I'm tempted to cave in and quit just like you are. But I'm still here, and I'm staying here to finish what we committed to do. We're going to get this thing done!" He was telling us that what we were doing was worth working hard for, worth fighting for, worth sacrificing for, and worth hurting for. In the face of pain and fatigue and loneliness and the temptation to quit, that kid hung in there to the end and kept calling us to do the same. His challenge left a deep imprint on everybody who heard him scream in agony, "Ahm sti heah! Ahm sti heah! Ahm sti heah!"

Here's what I'm saying: *Anything of great value is worth fighting for, sacrificing for, hurting for and even dying for. Don't cave in to the pressure and the pain. Keep believing, keep making a play, keep hanging in there, and never – never – give up!*

Avoiding the Easy Way Out

These days it seems so easy to give in, give up, and throw in the towel instead of following through with commitments and hanging in there for the long haul. Instead of yelling "Ahm sti heah!" in difficult situations, many people whisper "I'm outta here!" In the marriage ceremony couples commit to love and serve each other "till death do us part." But roughly half of all marriages in the U.S. today end in divorce as husbands and wives find it easier to say "We're not waiting till death—we're splittin' up while we're alive!" I sometimes think the reason many couples prefer early afternoon weddings is so if the marriage doesn't work out, they haven't wasted a whole day!

You can see this lack of commitment and perseverance everywhere you look. People give up on their jobs and either quit or change companies instead of toughing it out when the going gets tough. Many students avoid pushing themselves at school and opt for classes where the work is lighter and grades are easier to achieve. Some dads walk out on their wives and kids because family responsibilities interfere with their careers or sexual appetites. Parents use hobbies or sports or a hectic social life to divert them from the really tough work of investing time and energy in their kids day in and day out. And many church members won't sign up as volunteers because they consider the jobs menial, and these roles might require too much of their leisure time.

My response to this dilemma is that there are some things worth going the distance for, worth fighting for, worth sacrificing for, worth working harder for than you have ever worked in your life – and even worth dying for. There are some situations where we should stay and fight instead of cutting and running, hills we should be willing to die on because the causes are worth dying for. There are some tough jobs and roles in life where we need to say "Ahm sti heah!" instead of "I'm outta here!" Think of the great battles won and noble goals achieved because people made great plays of faith and refused to give up or give in. If we really want to demonstrate our belief in God and what is right, we will persevere to the end no matter what the cost.

The Bible is full of the stories of godly characters who endured much, suffered greatly and still cried out, "Ahm sti heah!" If we could hear their testimonies they might sound like this:

- Noah: "I've been building this monstrous boat in the desert for 120 years. There doesn't seem to be anything logical about this job, and I've been ridiculed and laughed at by my neighbors. But – Ahm sti heah!"
- Abraham and Sarah: "God told us twenty-five years ago that He would give us a son. We were old then and we're even older now. But we're not giving up. Wih sti heah!"
- Gideon: "God said that my army was too big, so he pared it down to 300. Going up against a much larger army this way seems crazy, but – Ahm sti heah!"
- Paul: "I've been through every kind of hardship you can imagine, and now I'm in a Roman prison and will probably be executed for my faith. But – Ahm sti heah!"
- Daniel: "I've been thrown into a cave with a pack of hungry lions because I wouldn't stop praying to God. These beasts should

have eaten me for dinner by now, but – Ahm sti heah!'"

- Stephen: "I'm lying here in this ditch being stoned by unbelievers because of my testimony for Jesus Christ, but – Ahm sti heah!'"
- Jesus: "I've been arrested, tried, convicted, crucified, buried and resurrected, but – Ahm sti heah!'"

Anything worthwhile we are called to do always seems to have an easy way out, a way to cut corners, loaf along, and avoid the hard work and pain. But this is not the Bible's way. If your faith prompts you to make a play of obedience and faithfulness, hang in there to the end. Wipe your face with the towel – but don't throw it in!

Enduring for the Joy of It

Here is a favorite scripture passage that gives us great motivation for determination and perseverance in living out our faith:

> *Therefore we also, since we are surrounded by so great a cloud of witnesses, let us lay aside every weight, and the sin which so easily ensnares us, and let us run with endurance the race that is set before us, looking unto Jesus, the author and finisher of our faith, who for the joy that was set before Him endured the cross, despising the shame, and has sat down at the right hand of the throne of God.*
>
> *For consider Him who endured such hostility from sinners against Himself, lest you become weary and discouraged in your souls.* (Hebrews 12:1-3)

The challenge of these verses is to long-term endurance. Endurance in this passage can also be translated "patience." It literally means to bare up under trials and tough times, to keep on keeping on even when the going gets tough. The first Christians to receive this letter were going through a time of great testing and were tempted to give up. The writer encourages them as well as us to hang tough just like Jesus, who endured the humiliation and suffering of the cross.

Then the writer reveals the secret of enduring and persevering through difficult circumstances, opposition and suffering. Jesus endured for "the joy that was set before him." Where could Jesus possibly find joy in being tortured and crucified? Well, first it was always His joy to do the will of the Father and to faithfully fulfill His assignment to the very end – death. Second, the joy for Jesus was the prospect of presenting His blameless church to the Father at the end of time. Finally, His joy was the anticipation of being seated at the right hand of the throne of God.

It may sound strange, but there is great joy awaiting you as you demonstrate belief through endurance, perseverance and even pain. The reason you can hang in there in the midst of trials and trouble is for the joy you will receive from honoring God, doing the right thing against opposition, finishing well, and knowing

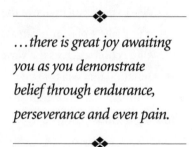

…there is great joy awaiting you as you demonstrate belief through endurance, perseverance and even pain.

you stayed true under pressure. There is also joy in knowing that a prize awaits you at the end of the race of endurance (1 Corinthians 9:24) and that your toil and effort will eventually be rewarded with great glory (2 Corinthians 4:16-18). It's worth it to endure a little hardship in this lifetime to receive joy and glory in heaven (Romans 8:18).

There's a great picture of "perseverance under pressure" in C.S. Lewis's fantasy tale, *Voyage of the Dawn Treader*. The ship was about to set sail on a journey to Aslan, the great lion in the Narnia series who symbolizes Jesus. But an approaching storm causes the sailors to abandon the launch. Reepicheep, a small but valiant warrior mouse, quietly climbs into a lifeboat on the side of the ship and begins to lower it to the water.

The crew cries out to him, "What are you going to do?"

"I'm going to sail to Aslan," the mouse replies.

"What will you do if the storm breaks your mast?"

"I'll row and row," answers Reepicheep.

"What if you lose your oars?"

"Then I'll get out of the boat and kick as hard as I can so I can reach my precious Aslan."

"What if your dingy sinks?"

"Then I'll swim and swim and hard as I can," the mouse insists.

"But what if you can't make it?"

"Then the rescuers will have to search for me, and if they are able, they will find my little body lying on the bottom of the ocean *with my head clearly pointed toward Aslan!*"

What a powerful image of the commitment and willingness to do whatever it takes to make a play. You can almost hear the sound of Reepicheep's squeaky little voice echoing across the waves – "Ahm sti heah-h-h-h!" This is the kind of determination that will get you through your commitments to your family, your work, your church, your ministry, and to "Aslan" – Jesus your Lord! Join me in shouting to the top of your voice for all the world to hear – "Ahm sti heah!"

That's a lesson about belief and perseverance from a mouse. In the next chapter, I'll share another powerful lesson about belief – from a goose.

17

Honk, if You Believe

At the start of Baylor's Fall football practice every year, we had to complete a twelve-minute run to show the coaches we were in shape. I hated the twelve-minute run. I wasn't that good of a runner to begin with, so the best I could do in twelve minutes was about seven laps around the track. I would stay in Waco with the other athletes all summer long getting in shape for the run. We all just hated it.

One hot summer day my teammate Tom Turnipseede and I happened to be running around the track at the same time, and soon we were running side by side. After a while we were in total sync. Our arms and legs were pumping in rhythm stride for stride. I mean, we were almost breathing together. It was incredible! We discovered how much easier it was to run together. The power we felt running side by side was unbelievable! When the day came to do the twelve-minute run, Tom and I ran the whole way side by side. And we did *over* seven laps. I'd never done that before!

I didn't realize what kind of energy Tom and I had tapped into, but many years later I read something that really opened my eyes about the power of teamwork. I was sitting in a dentist's office one day flipping through a copy of *Smithsonian Magazine* when I came across a fascinating article about geese. I went home and looked up some stuff about geese in the encyclopedia. I learned some incredible things about these big birds. What I learned about geese taught me a lot about how God designed people to get through trials and tough times and to fulfill His plans for their lives.

I'm going to share with you five things about geese that you can use in your life to get through tough stuff and reach the dreams God has planted in your heart. I call it the "Gospel According to a Goose."

1. Geese Fly in Formation

You've seen geese in the sky flying in that V formation. There's always a leader at the point and there are always two sides. That's how they fly. You may have also noticed that one side of the V is always longer than the other side. Do you know why? I mean, this is astounding! It's because there are more geese on the longer side. Isn't it amazing what you can learn from the encyclopedia?

Why do geese always fly in formation? Because they are committed to teamwork. Experts have discovered that geese fly 72 percent farther and more efficiently together than one goose can fly alone. They can fly over 1,000 miles at a time without stopping for rest if they fly as a team. The teamwork thing is also true for horses. One horse can pull a lot of weight, but you combine the strength and effort of two horses, and they can pull seven times what one horse can pull. And a whole team of horses (four to six) can pull twenty-four times what one horse can pull. Unbelievable! It's a matter of teamwork.

You need a team of people around you to help you succeed. And other people need you on their team in order for all to succeed.

It must be an awesome feeling for a goose that is flying in formation. What a rush to hear the steady sound of the wings flapping and feel the synergy and energy and dynamic of being in that flock. It has to be incredible! In fact, each goose in formation gets an aerodynamic lift from the bird in front of it. At times a bird will fall out of formation for some reason, and almost immediately it will realize, "Hey, it's a lot harder out here on my own. I'm getting back in formation!"

Here's a great insight from geese: *Living out God's plan for you in the midst of life's difficulties and challenges is difficult – you don't need to go it alone.* You need a team of people around you to help you succeed. And other people need you on their team in order for all to succeed.

The Bible tells us that God designed people to live and work more efficiently together than apart. After creating Adam, God said, "It is not good that man should be alone" (Genesis 2:18). The first woman was given to the first man, and together Adam and Eve became the first team.

God's intention from the very beginning was for a man and woman in a marriage relationship to be a team that edifies and blesses both of their lives. That's why it is sad to see so many couples not functioning as a team. God also wants you and your work associates to function as a team. You know, some work situations are just a drag – no energy, no sense of teamwork, no fun. Yet other coworkers seem to exude energy and dynamic when they are together. They're the ones who get things done and are excited about doing them together.

You can see the beauty of the team in the words of Ecclesiastes 4:9-12:

Two are better than one; because they have a good reward for their labor.
For if they fall, one will lift up his companion.
But woe to him who is alone when he falls,
for he has no one to help him up.
Again, if two lie down together, they will keep warm;
but how can one be warm alone?
Though one may be overpowered by another,
two can withstand him.
And a threefold cord is not quickly broken.

These verses can refer to any kind of relationship: a marriage, a family, a close friendship, a group of coworkers, or even a couple of college guys trying to conquer the twelve-minute run. These verses remind me of the acrostic someone came up with for TEAM: Together Everyone Achieves More.

When I was a senior at Baylor, our football team won the conference championship after many years of losing seasons. As the victories kept coming that season, we realized, "Hey, this is big. We have a chance to do something that hasn't been done at Baylor in fifty years. We could win a championship!" All through that season we were fired up because we were part of something big, and that's what it means to be a team.

Is there anything in your life that you are part of today that's bigger than you are, something that improves the quality of your life and gives you a perspective of being part of something huge? I get that feeling when I think about being part of my church. I say to myself, "This is big. I'm part of something that is way bigger than I am. What this church is doing is larger than what I or any one person could ever do alone." For example, every year we have huge musical programs that draw thousands of people. Dozens of athletic teams involve boys and girls of all ages in sports – and all of them get to play. The Fall Festival in late October draws between 15,000 and 20,000 children and parents for a night of excitement and fun. These and hundreds of classes, Bible studies, services and special events require thousands of people working as a team to make incredible things happen. It's impossible to be a part of it and not revel in the thought that it's "bigger than I am!"

> *What this church is doing is larger than what I or any one person could ever do alone.*

The sense of team is why I'm proud to be a Christian and a member of the Kingdom of God. I'm not only part of something much bigger that I am, I'm part of something that will outlast my seventy or eighty years on this planet. God's kingdom existed in eternity past and will continue into eternity future. Millions and millions of people are part of this team that exists to worship God and be witnesses of His love on earth. I am fired up about being a Christian on such an incredible team!

Everybody is in a family. You have an earthly family, and I pray that the kids, parents, spouses, grandpas and grandmas in your family build up and enjoy and support each other like a true team. If you have trusted Jesus Christ as your Savior, you also have a spiritual family here on earth. It's important to connect with this family on a regular basis to worship, study the Word, pray for each other, and support each other as you follow Christ together. And you have a home in heaven with a heavenly family where you will spend eternity with God. Won't it be incredible to get together in heaven with our great Team Leader?

Just like a goose, you were not created to fly alone. You need a team around you to help you hang in there through the journey and succeed at what God has called you to do. You can always go farther and accomplish more as a team.

2. Every Goose Is a Leader

When geese fly in formation, it seems like they have only one leader: the goose out front. But the lead goose has a huge, tiring job slicing through the wind at the head of the flock. When he gets weary, he drops back and another goose moves up to take his place. In a flock of geese, every goose takes a turn at the point – therefore every goose in the flock is a leader. Every goose has to show up and make a play!

Let me encourage you: Everyone is a leader, including you, and you need to take your turn leading. Your reaction may be, "I don't think so, Neal. There's nothing special about me. I'm not a leader." You see, we have this idea that "leader" means being the president of something, being the main guy or main gal in charge of everybody, the one who has the most power, the biggest position and the biggest office. But we need to realize that everybody is a leader because everybody has a platform and a sphere of influence where he or she can lead. In your circle of influence, whether it's large or small, you need to step up and lead because everybody is a leader.

We are in a crisis of leadership in America, especially in places like government and big business. But I believe our greatest leadership crisis is in the home. Too many moms and dads who are supposed to be leaders in the family are just not stepping up to lead. If you are a parent, your kids are depending on you to lead them. Get up front on the point and lead!

The book of Exodus tells the story of a great, great leader – Moses. Moses did one of the most significant things in human history when he led 2-3 million Jews out of Egypt. Incredible task! The logistics alone are mind-boggling. What a leader! But before he did that, do you know what he was doing? He was leading sheep on the backside of nowhere. Yet he was faithful in the task of leading those sheep, and in a burning bush experience he encountered God who told him, "Moses, I've seen the problems of your people Israel. And you're the man I'm going to use to lead these people out of bondage." Moses was up to the task all right – he led those 2-3 million Jews out of captivity, but he did it only after putting in some time leading a flock of sheep. He led his flock so well that God promoted him to lead millions of His people and go down in history as one of the greatest leaders of all time.

Maybe you would like to have a great position of leadership with more authority in your company. But if you're not leading faithfully in the small areas of responsibility now, you're not likely to get a shot at bigger things. Luke 16:10 says, "He who is faithful in what is least is faithful also in much; and he who is unjust in what is least is unjust also in much." This means that you are to lead where you are right now: at home, at work, at school, wherever. Take the position you've been placed in and go for it! If you are a leader, don't stand around looking at your shoes! Lead! If you don't step up to the plate and take a swing at the ball, you'll never have a chance to hit one out of the park. The point is this: lead where you are! If you're the head of your homeowner's association, lead! If you're an officer in a women's service club, lead! If you're captain of your high school drill team, lead! If you're serving as a "big brother" or "big sister" to a little guy or little girl in a poor neighborhood, lead! If you're a youth counselor at a summer camp for kids, lead! I promise that God will bless you and enlarge your sphere of influence as you lead where you are.

One thing you want to be sure of, though, is that you're leading in the right direction. Too many leaders today are going in the wrong direction because they are leading in ungodly ways. If you're going to lead, make sure everyone following you ends up in the right place – a good place, a godly place, a place you can be proud of.

3. Geese Honk to Encourage

Geese are honkers. When they honk, they are encouraging each other. It's the geese in the back of the flock that are honking at those in front. Do you know what they're saying when they honk? They're saying, "You can do it, guys! Keep flapping! We're with you! Hang in there! Good job! We're behind you!"

Here's what the geese are showing us: Everybody needs to be a honker because everybody needs to be encouraged. Everybody experiences tough times. At times everybody can feel badly about themselves. Everybody is hurting in some way. A teen gets dumped by a boyfriend or

❖

Everybody needs to be a honker because everybody needs to be encouraged.

❖

girlfriend or is struggling with grades. Someone is overworked and exhausted. Someone is experiencing marriage problems. You may see some folks you think have it all together, but I can promise you this – they need a honk, too. Why? Because everybody needs to be encouraged.

You know what the problem is? We're all waiting for someone to come along and encourage *us*! We get so down and depressed and focused on our problems that all we're doing is thinking how bad our life is. We become so inward-focused that depression and discouragement set in. But I promise you – if you turn away from your own problems and see what everyone else is struggling with, you'll realize that you've got it pretty good. You're not nearly as bad off as some other people, and other people need encouragement even more than you do. So get your eyes off yourself and find somebody you can honk at because they need encouragement. There are people who love you dearly – a wife or husband, a child, a mom or dad, a brother or sister, a friend – who just need to be encouraged. Give them a honk!

I read a story about a kid who was in the seventh grade. Nobody at school really knew this guy because he was kind of a loner. One day he got off the bus on his way home and dropped his book bag. Books and papers went everywhere. One of the other kids stopped and helped him pick up his stuff. They started walking and talking, and the loner kid asked the other kid to go home with him. So he went home with him, and they spent a couple of hours talking. Years later these two guys graduated from high school. The kid who had dropped his books told the other kid, "The day you helped me pick up my books, I was on my way home to end my life. I had nothing worth living for. And then, there you were to help me, walk alongside me, and even come to my house and spend some time with me. You know what? You saved my life." Now that's what I'm talking about! That's a honk!

A few years ago I gave a pep talk to the Baylor men's soccer team before they played a regional finals match. I talked to them about how geese fly together and encourage each other. Then I demonstrated a loud goose honk for them and had all the team members honking like geese in the locker room. It was fun and they were encouraged as they went out to play the match.

The game ended in a tie, so there was a penalty shoot-out to decide the winner. The other team went first and scored a point. Then our guy from Baylor put the ball down and stepped back to determine how he could get the ball past the goalie. It was a big pressure situation. If he missed the kick, the match was over and Baylor was out of the playoffs.

Suddenly, one of his teammates on the sideline let out a big goose honk! Then all the Baylor players started honking. Soon the parents and spectators in the stands were honking, even though they had no idea what it meant. Before long everyone on the Baylor side was honking their hearts out like a flock of wild geese. It was incredible! Well, we won that game, and I'm convinced it was because of the power of the honk.

Everybody needs to be encouraged, so honk!

4. Geese Stay Together In Good Times and Bad

When a goose gets sick or injured and settles to the ground, two other geese always leave the flock to stay with the downed goose until it can fly again or until it dies. Now these two geese have their own agenda: "Hey, we've got a schedule to keep. We've got places to go, things to do, geese to see. We've got to

Honk, if You Believe

hustle." But when another goose is in need, they detour from their set agenda, leave the formation and stay with their needy friend until the situation is over. That's a great picture of love and loyalty!

Jesus gave an even better picture of love and compassion in the parable of the Good Samaritan (Luke 10:25-37). A Jewish guy on a journey gets jumped, beaten up and robbed by thugs. A couple of Jewish religious leaders find him lying half dead by the side of the road; but because they have their own agendas, they just pass on by without doing anything to help the poor guy. Then the original Good Samaritan – actually from Samaria – comes along. Samaritans and Jews hated each other, but this Samaritan compassionately gives first aid to the victim and then makes sure he recovers fully. In the story, Jesus was saying that we are to show mercy and compassion to anyone who is hurting.

One of the amazing things about being in a family or a close friendship or a Bible study group is that over the long haul you experience what love really is. Love doesn't mean everything is always perfect and easy. There are always tough times and struggles. But it's in the midst of these struggles that you discover what your team means to you. This was true for Tom and me during those grueling laps together on the Baylor track. Some of those summer days were pure torture, but we stayed with each other until the very end.

One day a mother told her four-year-old son that their elderly neighbor had died and that her husband was now alone. Later that day the little boy saw the old man sitting in his back yard crying. The little guy went next door and climbed into the man's lap. Later his mother asked him what he said to their sad neighbor. He answered, "Nothing, I just helped him cry." That's love in action. It's so easy, even a four-year-old can do it!

How much did the rich man leave? He left it all. He may now be the richest man in the graveyard.

Whenever my teammates get together for a 1974 conference championship reunion, it's like we never left school. I've never experienced anything like it. There is love and unity in that room even after all those years. Why? Because we all won together, lost together, fought together, cried together and bled together. We experienced the good times and bad times together. And all those things experienced together by teams and families and friends and churches have a way of bringing hearts together as one.

If we consistently show devotion and compassion toward others who are going through tough times, we will make a positive mark on the world that nothing can erase.

5. Geese Always Complete the Journey

The flock travels thousands of miles with no navigation system and no computer – only what's built into them – and they always get where they're supposed to go. They experience victory at the end of the journey. God has wired into each goose the ability to succeed – to reach its final destination.

I want you to realize something: *God has also wired you to be victorious, to win and to succeed.* We usually see success as something like pulling straight A's in school, making a lot of money, having our own business, getting a promotion, keeping an orderly home or winning a championship. Those are types of success that are certainly worth pursuing, but they are not the ultimate victory. Ultimate victories are those things that last forever: Christian witness, the Word of God, good deeds in the lives of people around you, and making a difference on this earth.

Maybe you lose every match on your high school tennis team and struggle just to get C's, but you are a huge winner in life if you respect your parents and love your brothers and sisters. You will experience ultimate victory as a caring, supportive spouse and parent even if the rest of your world falls apart. If you never get that big promotion at work, but faithfully live out your faith in Jesus in front of your coworkers, you're a big winner in life. You can be victorious in life because you know the Creator of life – Jesus – who achieved nothing that today's world would call success, but who is the ultimate Victor of all time and eternity.

A lot of people experience great victories in areas such as academics, politics, business, sports, and finance, but when they get to the end of their life, they have lost. Why? Because they missed the ultimate victory of living for eternity. Everything they worked for and valued so highly died with them. How much did the rich man leave? He left it all. He may now be the richest man in the graveyard.

There is a God-shaped emptiness in everyone's heart that can be filled only by God himself. If you want to experience ultimate success at the end of your journey, you don't need a GPS or a Google map. You need to let God occupy His rightful place at the very center of your life. You need to live out His Word wherever you go and in all of your relationships. Only with Him will you be victorious.

There's another vital source of power for the journey as you live out your dreams and follow God's plans for your life. Section VI is all about the greatest force in the universe.

VI

THE GREATEST FORCE IN THE UNIVERSE
How to View and Value the Power of Love

And now abide faith, hope, love, these three;
but the greatest of these is love.
1 CORINTHIANS 13:13

Christian love, either towards God or towards man, is
an affair of the will.
C.S. LEWIS

18

A Love that Can't Be Stopped

As a kid and teenager, I struggled with feeling that I was not worthy to be loved for who I was. My stuttering caused me to feel inferior. I had a difficult time believing that anybody would accept me as a person of worth and value because, basically, I didn't believe I was a person of worth and value. I couldn't talk, and when I tried to talk, I sounded bad and looked ugly. From an early age, I concluded that no one could love and accept me as a stutterer.

But I still desperately needed the love and acceptance of my peers, so I assumed I had to perform to earn it. I was driven to do something that would convince my friends that I was someone worth loving. For me, that something was sports. I rationalized that if I excelled on the field and my peers accepted me for my achievements in sports, I might be able to accept myself. Well, I experienced success in sports and was respected as a good football player, but you know what? I still stuttered! I still couldn't talk. I still struggled with feelings of unworthiness and felt like I had to perform.

Do you know the big problem with performing to be loved? It's that you have to keep *performing* to be loved. And if you ever stop performing or if you lose your ability to perform, you feel like you've lost your reason to be loved. That's why a lot of professional athletes past their prime have such a hard time figuring out who they are. Since their self-image is defined by being the best on the field or court and by winning championships and making tons of money in sports, when age or injuries rob them of their abilities, they wind up losing their sense of identity and don't know where they fit in.

A huge thing happened to me when I was a sophomore in high school. I mean, it was life-changing! I discovered the amazing truth that began to transform the way I saw myself. I realized for the first time that Jesus Christ loved me just the way I was. As a kid going to Sunday school and church, I had heard the message of God's love for me many, many times, but when I was sixteen that message finally got through to me. I was loved by God not because I was a good football player or for anything else I had done, could do, or would ever do. God loved me just the way I was – as a stutterer. The power of God's love totally changed my life!

The Awesome Power of Love

I didn't date a whole lot in high school. I mean, it's just hard to stutter and be cool at the same time. I was scared to death of girls. I couldn't talk when I was around them. In my mind there was no way a girl would love a guy like me. And on the rare dates I did have during high school, my whole focus was to hide the fact that I stuttered. I thought, "As soon as she hears me talk, she's out of here for sure." So I just wouldn't talk.

When I went to pick her up at the dorm and saw her for the first time, my thought was, "I am way out of my league here. I have no shot with a girl this beautiful. And as soon as she hears me talk, it'll be all over."

I met my wife Sheila on a blind date at Baylor. When I went to pick her up at the dorm and saw her for the first time, my thought was, "I am way out of my league here. I have no shot with a girl this beautiful. And as soon as she hears me talk, it'll be all over." But we did talk, and when I asked Sheila out again she said yes. I couldn't believe it! As we continued dating, I grew to like her a lot. She was a special, godly girl and she said she liked me, too. My thought was, *Yeah, right. You may like me, but there's no way you're going to love me and want to marry me.*

Remember how it was when you were dating – or how it is if you're dating now? You're afraid to show your true self, so you always put your best side forward and try to hide the rest. Why is that? Because you're afraid that if people see you the way you really are – that your feet smell, you snore, you're snarly in the morning and so on – they won't like you. It all comes back to that basic fear that people won't love you just the way you are.

Well, words can't describe how I felt on February 7, 1976, when I stood at the altar of the First Baptist Church in Wylie, Texas, and gazed down the aisle to see Sheila standing at the back with her dad. The music started and her dad escorted her down the aisle to stand beside me. Then in front of the preacher and the congregation and God, she said in essence, "Neal, I know everything about you – the good, the bad, and the ugly. I know all that stuff about you. But none of it matters to me. I love you and I choose you as the man I will spend the rest of my life with."

Can you imagine how powerful that moment was for a guy who never thought it would happen to him? The awesome power of Sheila's love has changed my life because I know she loves me just as I am. I know that I am a person of worth and value because I have been touched by the transforming power of love of the God who saved me and the beautiful woman who chose me above all others.

Here's what I want you to get: *Love is the greatest motivating force in the world. People who know that they are loved just for who they are – even with their weaknesses and faults – cannot be stopped in whatever they set out to do.* Money is a great motivator in life, but it can only take you so far. Fear is a huge motivator, but love can wipe it out. Unconditional love takes you all the way. Power and position and a great career are fine and have their place, but nothing makes a greater impact on the human heart and human behavior than knowing you are totally loved.

God loves you unconditionally just the way you are. You don't have to perform for His love because there is nothing you can do that will make Him love you. You don't have to work for it because no amount of achievement will make Him love you. And you don't have to pay for it because His love is completely free. All you can do is accept His love and thank Him for it with a life of love and service.

You may say, "Neal, give me one good reason why the God of the universe could possibly love me just as I am." Well, I can do better than that. I can give you three incredible reasons why God loves and values you unconditionally. These are the same three things that caused me to realize in high school that God loved and valued me just for being me.

God Created You

First, *God loves you because He made you.* You are the creative work of an awesome God in heaven. King David got pretty excited about this fact. He wrote, "I will praise You, for I am fearfully and wonderfully made; marvelous are Your works, and that my soul knows very well" (Psalm 139:14). As God's special work of art, you are automatically a person of great worth and value because, as the old saying goes, God don't make no junk!

This concept of the Creator loving His creation really clicked for me when my wife and I had our first child. On August 3, 1980, Sheila woke me up in the middle of the night and said "We're about to have a baby!" We got in the car and rushed to the hospital. After twelve hours – finally – at 12:06 p.m. on August 3, I watched the most incredible thing I've ever seen in my life: the birth of our first child, Natalie Marie Jeffrey. In the years following, I watched the birth of our other two kids, Melissa and James, and it blew me away every time. It's unthinkable to me how anyone can watch the birth of a new baby and not believe that there is a great God in heaven.

There I was, twenty-seven years old at the time and holding this little 7 pound, 10 ounce baby. And here's what I thought: This little baby has never seen me before; she has no idea who I am. She hasn't done anything for me yet – made good grades, said "Daddy, I love you," hugged my neck or kissed me on the cheek. Yet next to my wife Sheila, she was the most valuable, precious thing on the face of the earth to me, and I loved her with all my heart. You know why? Because I helped make her and *she was mine through creation!*

Now if a sinful human father can feel that kind of love for a child who has done nothing to earn his love, imagine how a perfect, loving God in heaven feels about you. He says about you, "You're mine because I created you." That's incredible! God doesn't love you for what you do or don't do. He doesn't love you because of how good or successful you are. And He doesn't withhold His love based on your lack of goodness or success. God loves you because He created you, and you will always be loved by God because you will always be His creation. In fact, even if you never say yes to Jesus Christ but choose to spend your life in rebellion against Him, He still loves you. As God's personal creation, you are a person of ultimate worth and value to Him.

Jesus Died for You

The second thing that reveals how much God loves you is that *Jesus died for you.* No verse in the Bible says it any plainer than John 3:16: "God so loved the world that He gave His only begotten Son, that whoever believes in Him should not perish but have everlasting life." I love reading the verse this way, "God so loved Neal Jeffrey that He gave His only begotten Son, that because Neal Jeffrey believes in Him he should not perish but have everlasting life." Go ahead, read the verse again with your name in it. You'll love the way it sounds!

Why did He die for you and me? Because all of us are sinners in need of a Savior. It's one of the common denominators of every person who has ever lived. As Paul wrote, "All have sinned and fall short of the glory of God" (Romans 3:23). All of us are moral failures. All of us are guilty of rebelling against the God who created us and values us. All of us have violated God's law. All of us have done what God says not to do. So all of us have a sin problem, which means we also have a death problem. Romans 6:23 says, "The wages of sin is death." God loves you, but He can't tolerate sin. So He must separate Himself from the sinner. Our sin has earned for us eternal separation from God, which is death.

Since you have a sin problem and a death problem, you need a Savior. But God your Creator loves you totally, so He provided the Savior you need. God sent His perfect and sinless Son Jesus from heaven to earth. He was born to a virgin named Mary, lived a perfect life, and then went to the cross in your place. The spotless Lamb of God died on the cross to pay for your sin. The wrath you deserved because of your sin was placed on Him. All the terrible things that should have happened to you happened to Him instead.

If you saw the movie *The Passion of the Christ*, you have some idea of how horrible His death really was. It was very difficult for me to watch the graphic portrayal of Jesus suffering the brutal blows with fists and sticks and whips, and see the torn flesh and spilled blood. Why did He do it? Because He loves you and me enough to become the Savior we need. What had we done to deserve His loving sacrifice? Absolutely nothing. In fact, we deserve the treatment that Jesus received. Romans 5:8 says, "God demonstrates His own love toward us, in that while we were still sinners, Christ died for us."

You know what? You get so much because of what Jesus did for you on the cross. You get forgiveness of sin. You get meaning, purpose and peace in life. You get heaven and eternity with God. In fact, you get everything God is and has! It's all free to you, but it cost God everything for you to have it. It cost God the death of His only Son. Every time you see a cross – on a church, on a necklace, in a painting, anywhere – it should remind you that Jesus gave His life for you because He loves you.

God Chose You

Here's the third reason why you can know that God loves you and values you: *He chose you.* God has a plan for your life, something He wants you to do. His plan for you is part of His overall plan for the world, and He selected you for a special role in it. You can think of it this way: "God has a team, and He has picked me to be on it. He looked around at everyone and said, 'Hey, I choose you!'"

Do you know how it feels *not* to get picked for something? Maybe you tried out for a sport or auditioned for a part in the school play or applied for a cool job or ran for a political office in school or community. But you didn't make it, you weren't selected, you were passed by. How did you feel? You probably felt unwanted, unloved, incapable, inferior, or like you just weren't quite good enough. But God says, "I love you. You're good enough for *me*. I have something just right for you to do. I choose *you* on my team!"

When I was growing up in Kansas, we had a great house with a half-acre backyard. My neighborhood buddies and I played football in my backyard just about every day. I mean, we had so much fun it was incredible! Kids would start showing up and hanging out on our patio. Then we would select two captains and choose up teams. Then the game was on.

Well, we had a guy in our neighborhood named George who was smaller than everyone else and slow in every sense of the word. And George was a terrible football player. He always showed up, but he was so bad that nobody wanted him on their team. Everybody would be on the patio while the captains chose teams, but George sat on a big rock next to the garage and he was never chosen. Then we all ran out to play the game, and George would kind of mosey out there with us. Eventually, one of the teams would give in and let George play.

One day the whole neighborhood showed up to play football as usual. This time my big cousin James was there to play with us. Most of the kids who played were in the sixth or seventh grade, but James was in high school, so he got to be first captain. We were all milling around the patio and George is out there on his rock. And James, with his first pick, took George. Well, George was so shocked he fell off his rock! And the rest of us were blown away! George had never been picked before, but that day he was the number one pick!

We literally saw in that moment an amazing transformation. George picked himself up and walked through all these guys who hadn't been picked yet. I mean, his head was high, his shoulders were back, his chest was out. He strutted through the whole gang like he was the king of the world until he was standing behind James. His proud look and strut said it all: "I've been chosen!"

You have every right to feel the same way George felt. Why? Because God created you, sent his Son to die for you, and chose you to be on His team. You didn't deserve to be picked by God any more than George deserved to be the first pick for our game that day. But God doesn't love you for what you can do; He loves you for who you are. And He picked you!

When each one of our three kids was a baby, every night at bedtime I would rock them, sing to them and say things like, "Daddy loves you. Mommy loves you. Jesus loves you." As they grew older and started to talk, the bedtime ritual changed a little. Instead of listing the people that loved them, I would ask, "Who loves you?" And each kid was delighted to recite the list for me: Daddy, Mommy, Jesus, Grandpa, Grandma and so on.

Well, one night when I was rocking and singing to our second daughter, I said, "Melissa, who loves you?" She looked straight at me and said, "Mr. Rogers." It blew me away! I knew she watched the kids' program *Mr. Rogers' Neighborhood* on TV. All our kids did. But I had never put Mr. Rogers on my bedtime list of people who loved her. I was a little puzzled about how he got on Melissa's list. But as I thought about it, it made perfect sense. Every day as Mr. Rogers changed his shoes and put on his jacket to leave, he looked right at Melissa and said things like, "I think you're special. I like you just the way you are. I'll come back to see you tomorrow." Melissa was totally convinced that Mr. Rogers loved her. No wonder he made my little girl's list!

You know, when you're convinced that the great God of heaven loves you just as you are, you can endure any trial, rise above any obstacle, survive any defeat, and accomplish significant things for God. Why? Because you have the greatest power in the universe on your side! You are loved even though you aren't perfect. You are loved even if you lose the game. You are loved even if everybody around you thinks you're a failure. With this kind of power behind you, you are unstoppable!

It's one thing to know about the transforming power of love; it's another thing to experience it and be transformed by it. The next chapter zeroes in on this amazing transformation.

19

Plug into the Hug

For Baylor folks, the day we beat Texas for the conference championship is still the greatest victory of all time! I mean, it's a major deal to beat Texas any time, but to beat them with the championship on the line is incredible! I still have a poster of the scoreboard showing the final score – Baylor 34, Texas 24. And I still have a video of the game that I'm happy to show to anyone who wants to see it! That was my best game as a quarterback and an athlete. I was the hero of the moment. *Sports Illustrated* named me Offensive Back of the Week for leading the comeback victory.

But my greatest thrill that day was walking out of the locker room after the game and seeing my dad there waiting for me. Dad was my hero, a big man, a real man's man, a former Baylor football player with huge arms and shoulders. He walked up to me after the game as he always did and gave me a big old bear hug. In that hug he said it all: "Son, I love you, I'm proud of you, you were incredible." It was everything a boy dreams about: being the hero of the big game with your dad watching and then being showered with his affection and approval in a manly bear hug.

Nowhere else can you see the power of love more clearly demonstrated than in a big bear hug. The hug seems to be one of those universal signs of love and affection that says something words can't say. If you haven't seen your mom or dad or son or daughter in a while, don't you give them a big hug when you see them? Go to the airport and you see people hugging everywhere. Travelers returning from a trip are smothered with hugs from their family and friends that say, "Welcome home. I missed you. I'm glad you're home safe." And some of the most heart-touching hugs are when people are leaving on a long trip or moving away. Those hugs say, "I'm so sad to see you go. I miss you already."

It may sound like an old fashioned word, but I think "beloved" is a great way to explain what is being said in a hug. A person who is beloved to you is someone who is near and dear to your heart. In fact, when you're hugging someone, your two hearts are about as close to each other as they can get. In the Old Testament, David and Jonathan had a strong, loving and manly friendship. They were big huggers. Their relationship is described this way: "The soul of Jonathan was knit to the soul of David, and Jonathan loved him as his own soul" (1 Samuel 18:1). In the same way, our hugs say, "I love you, I appreciate you, I value you. You are dear to my heart – you are beloved."

Living in the Hug

I want to show you two incredible things in the Bible about "beloved." The first one is in Matthew 3. It's at the beginning of Jesus' ministry and He has just been baptized by John the Baptist. When Jesus came up out of the water, an amazing thing happened: "Suddenly a voice came from heaven, saying, 'This is My beloved Son, in whom I am well pleased'" (v.17).

Whose voice was it? It was God the Father's voice. Who was He talking about? His Son Jesus, calling Him "My beloved Son." Wrapped up in that word "beloved" are all the love and unity and oneness and acceptance that the Father has for His Son. It's as if the Father is reaching down from heaven to throw His arms around Jesus in a big bear hug. And in that hug God is saying, "I love you, Son. You're the joy of my heart. I'm so proud of you." There is such awesome love and oneness in the relationship between the Father and the Son. They actually live "in the hug."

The second thing I want to show you in the Bible about beloved was written by the Apostle Paul. He described to the Christians in Ephesus some of the incredible blessings God provides for those who trust Jesus Christ as Savior:

> He [God] chose us in Him before the foundation of the world, that we should be holy and without blame before Him in love, having predestined us to adoption as sons by Jesus Christ to Himself, according to the good pleasure of His will, to the praise of the glory of His grace, by which <u>He made us accepted in the beloved</u>. (Ephesians 1:4-6; emphasis is mine)

Look at that last phrase again, "By which He made us accepted *in the beloved*." Do you realize what that phrase is saying? It's saying that since God the Father and Jesus are in the hug, you as a believer in Jesus are in the hug as well. You are in the beloved with the Father and the Son! Picture this: God the Father and Jesus the Son are locked in a big, loving bear hug, and you are right in the middle of that hug! You're surrounded by the Father's love for His Son and by Jesus' love for His Father. That's what it means to be "in the beloved."

Here's the point: If you have trusted Jesus as your Savior, you live in that hug every day. You are constantly surrounded by the love of God. You didn't get there by scoring enough points or by doing enough good deeds. You're in that hug because of God's love for you expressed through Jesus and your love for God expressed through faith.

You're in that hug because of God's love for you expressed through Jesus and your love for God expressed through faith.

Do you realize how powerful it is to be wrapped in God's bear hug every moment of every day of your life – and then through eternity? I mean, what do you ever have to be afraid of? Nothing! The only things that can get to you inside that hug are things God allows to build your character and make you stronger. If kids at school blow you off because of your walk with Jesus, you and your hurt feelings are safe inside the hug. If you are dealing with cancer, you and your cancer are sheltered inside the hug. If you experience a personal tragedy or if your child is in rebellion or you have been falsely accused of something by someone, you and everything that touches you are surrounded by the "everlasting arms" of God's hug.

And God is never going to let you go. Paul writes, "I am persuaded that neither death nor life, nor angels nor principalities nor powers, nor things present nor things to come, nor height nor depth, nor any other created thing, shall be able to separate us from the love of God which is in Christ Jesus our Lord" (Romans 8:38-39).

But there's more to being in the hug than the power and peace and provision we get out of it. God has long arms and a lot of love to share, and it's up to us to share it.

Living out the Hug

Jesus told his disciples, "A new commandment I give to you, that you love one another; as I have loved you, that you also love one another" (John 13:34). The power you gain from living in the hug of God's love is not just for you but for everybody around you. God wants you to demonstrate how much his love has changed your life but pulling others into the hug wherever you go.

Jesus went on to say, "By this all will know that you are My disciples, if you have love for one another" (v.35). What's He talking about? He means that our love for one another will be the convincing proof that we are His followers. Our greatest witness to the watching world is not how big our churches are or the sayings we put on the marquis out front or the number of tracts we pass out or how many Bibles we give away – as good as these things may be. Rather, when the world sees how we include each other in the hug every day they will say, 'Whoa! Look how they care for each other. All the stuff they say about Jesus must be true!"

The New Testament gives us a lot practical ways to demonstrate that we are "in the beloved" in our relationships. Here are several of them.

Get a grip on others. The early Christians were a "touchy-feely" bunch of people in the best sense of the word. Paul wrote things like, "Be kindly affectionate to one another with brotherly love" (Romans 12:10) and "Greet one another with a holy kiss" (Romans 16:16). These verses are talking about brotherly love and family love, not romantic or sexual love. He's saying that being in the hug of God's love ought to show up in the warm physical affection we show one another.

Now, I don't think this means you have to literally hug or kiss everyone in your church. But you can convey a lot of love to others through warm expressions of brotherly love such as a firm handshake, a pat on the back or the arm, a strong grip around the shoulders, a big bear hug, and even a brotherly or sisterly kiss on the cheek when it's appropriate.

Make room for differences. Do you realize how many different kinds of people are included in the beloved? You can get an idea by looking at the list of different ethnic groups in Jerusalem when 3,000 people were saved (see Acts 2:5-11). Can you imagine what some of those early congregations of new Christians looked like? People of different colors and different languages and different histories and traditions were among those who heard Peter's sermon, believed and were baptized. You could go to church and have a Parthian and an Arab sitting on either side of you with a couple of Elamites in front of you. What a melting pot of different kinds of people!

You know, we tend to hang out with people who are most like us, and we tend to keep a distance from those who are different from us. I guess that's why Paul wrote, "Accept one another, then, just as Christ accepted you" (Romans 15:7 NIV). God's love has a wide reach that embraces a world of differences. He welcomes into the hug *all* who trust in His Son, no matter who they are or where they are in life. I mean, get a clue! Look at what He got when He accepted you into the hug! If we don't accept everyone Jesus accepts, no matter how different they may be, the world can rightly say of us, "That Jesus stuff is bogus."

Take up the towel. One of the last things Jesus did with his disciples was to wash their feet. It was the job of a common servant to rinse and dry a guest's dusty feet, but Jesus took up the towel and did a servant's job. Then He said, "If I then, your Lord and Teacher, have washed your feet, you also ought to wash one another's feet. For I have given you an example, that you should do as I have done to you" (John 13:14-15).

You may say, "I'm glad that command was just for the disciples in the upper room. Being a servant sounds like an awful job." Well, Jesus meant it for all His followers. Paul explains, "Through love serve one another" (Galatians 5:13). That verse could literally read, "Be each other's slaves." In other words, being in the hug with others means that we all assume the servant's role from time to time.

Keep your eyes open for the needs of the people around you. And when you find a need, see what you can do to meet that need. A friend in your youth group is struggling with a science project, so you offer to help her out. The chairs need to be folded up after Bible study, so you stay ten minutes to get it done. You volunteer to watch a friend's preschooler while she goes to her doctor's appointment. Whenever you see someone in need, just think about Jesus kneeling down to wash the disciples' feet. If you had been in that room, He would have washed your feet. Now what can you do to serve those you see in need?

Paul also tells us, "Submit to one another out of reverence to Christ" (Ephesians 5:21 NIV). "Submit" is another servant word. It means that you don't always have to be the boss in every situation. OK, so it's your little brother's job to feed the family pets every night after dinner. Would it kill you to do it for him when you see that he has a huge load of homework to start on? Serving others is an expression of your love for Jesus who did more for you than you can ever repay.

Let people off the hook. Do you realize that all believers in the hug of God's love – including you – are imperfect? Everybody has rough edges that rub people the wrong way. Everybody gets angry or hurt and says something that hurts or angers others. And everybody sins against God and wrongs people. What's more, God planned for us to live closely together – not separately like hermits who have no one to offend – but in families, as roommates in college, in church youth groups and Bible study groups and home fellowship groups, and so on. How are all these imperfect people supposed to get along?

Here's how the Bible answers that question: "Walk worthy of the calling with which you were called, with all lowliness and gentleness, with longsuffering, bearing with one another in love" (Ephesians 4:1-2); "Be kind to one another, tenderhearted, forgiving one another, even as God in Christ forgave you" (Ephesians 4:32). In other words, when people do you wrong in big ways or small, you *hug* them by hanging in there with them and forgiving them instead of giving up on them. Why? Because when your sin sent Jesus to the cross, that's how God responded to you. Martin Luther King Jr. said, "He who is devoid of the power to forgive is devoid of the power of love." Being in the hug means letting people off the hook when they bug us or wrong us in some way. As Josh McDowell says, "Forgiveness is the oil of relationships." Forgiveness keeps families, friendships, neighbors and churches running smoothly.

Hold each other accountable. The Bible calls Christians to "admonish one another" (Romans 15:14). To admonish means to hold people accountable for their actions, by warning them in a Christ-like way. If you see a Christian friend getting into behavior that's not right, you might admonish him or her by saying, "Are you sure this is the right thing for you to do? Can we talk and pray about it together?" Or maybe someone in your company is becoming overly critical of coworkers or policies in a way that is hurting morale, so you go to that person and admonish him or her. We're not talking about judging or condemning people or trying to make them feel bad. It's about caring enough that you step up and show concern if they appear to be straying off the path. It's the hug that holds others close in difficult times.

Be the "twelfth man." Texas A&M University is one of Baylor's major rivals in sports. Both schools are located on the Brazos River only ninety miles apart. During my four years at Baylor, the Aggies beat us three out of four times in football, including a 20-0 pounding the year we won the conference championship. The Aggies were extra tough to play in their home stadium at College Station because of the tradition called the "twelfth man."

Way back in 1922, the Aggies were big underdogs in a game against a top-ranked team. As the game wore on, a number of Aggie players were knocked out of the game with injuries. There were hardly any players left on the bench. Their coach, a guy with the interesting name of Dana X. Bible, remembered that a former player named E. King Gill was up in the press box working as a spotter.

Coach Bible called Gill down from the press box and asked him to suit up just in case he ran completely out of players.

When the game ended, which A&M won 22-14, Gill was the only man left standing on the sidelines for the Aggies – their "twelfth man." He never got into the game, but he stood ready to help in case his team needed him. His spirit of service, support and enthusiasm inspired a tradition at A&M that has continued to the present. At every football game, the A&M student body is called the Twelfth Man. They stand for the entire game to show their support of the team. The raucous cheers of the Twelfth Man have urged on the Aggie football team and tormented opposing teams like Baylor for more than eighty years.

The Bible tells us that being a "twelfth man" is one way we can keep one another in the hug. Hebrews 10:24 says, "Spur one another on toward love and good deeds" (NIV). And in 1 Thessalonians 5:11 we read, "Encourage one another and build each other up" (NIV). Those of us inside God's loving embrace are to be each other's biggest cheerleaders and supporters, celebrating victories and mourning defeats together. Like E. King Gill, we show our love for one another by standing ready to inspire and encourage each other as we follow Christ.

The Hug Never Lets You Go

In 1973, the year before my dream season at Baylor, we played Texas Christian University for homecoming. You want to play well in every game, of course, but the homecoming game is huge! You want to impress all the alumni who are in town for the big game on Saturday, so there is extra incentive to play a great game.

Well, with only eleven minutes left in the game we were getting killed, 34-7. But we got fired up and scored three quick touchdowns, cutting the Horned Frogs' lead to 34-28. The crowd went wild. All we had to do was get the ball one more time, drive the field for a touchdown and kick the extra point to win the game, 35-34. We accomplished the first part as our defense held TCU and we got the ball back at our own 25 yard line with a minute and a half left in the game. Then, miraculously, we marched down the field to the TCU 15 yard line with only 27 seconds left to score the touchdown.

When the ball was snapped, I hit one of our receivers in the flat near the sideline. The game film clearly showed that if our guy had zipped straight down the sideline after the catch he would have scored the winning touchdown. But for some reason – and I'm still in counseling for this – our guy caught the ball, turned back toward the middle of the field, and got tackled on the 12 yard line. Huge problem: The clock was ticking down and we had no more timeouts. I knew I had to quickly throw the ball out of bounds to stop the clock so we could set up the game-winning play.

And that's just what I did. I threw the ball out of bounds and stopped the clock. *Except it was fourth down.* Now if you're not that into football, throwing the ball out of bounds on fourth down is a major mistake because the other team automatically gets the ball. In my head, *I thought it was third down,* giving me one play to stop the clock and one more play to win the game. But when I threw the ball out of bounds, I threw the game away! TCU ran one more play as time expired and beat us, 34-28.

You can't imagine how awful I felt walking off a football field with 40,000 fans glaring down on me and each one of them thinking unchristian thoughts about me! I know what they were thinking because a lot of them wrote me letters the next week. I had made a huge mistake and my blunder cost us a come-from-behind homecoming victory. I was bitterly disappointed about bringing my teammates so close to victory and then literally throwing the game away. I sat in the locker room after the game and wept.

It is difficult to describe how I felt, walking out of the locker room that day. But there was my dad, just like always. He walked over to me as only my dad could, a man's man, a big man with those big hands and broad shoulders. And he gave me a big old bear hug. I was so devastated that I just buried my head on his shoulder and cried.

Here's what I want you to see: *On the greatest day of my life as an athlete when we beat Texas, and I was the hero, and I got the job done – you know what? – I got that hug. And on the worst day of my life as an athlete, when I blew it, when*

I was the goat, when I made the mistake that cost us the game, when I failed — you know what? — I still got that hug! There were two completely opposite results in those big games, but I got the exact same hug from my dad. *That's the power of love!* That's God's love expressed through the love of His people.

Every person alive needs a hug, needs to feel loved just as they are, needs to know they are valued. Teenager, your mom and dad need a hug from you. Hey, I know you have differences, and they may not understand you the way you want them to. But that doesn't matter. Give them a hug to show that you love them no matter what. Husband or wife, your spouse needs a hug with no strings attached, one that simply expresses your deep love and lasting commitment. Parent, your kids need your arms wrapped around them often, assuring them that you love them just as they are.

Your hugs are a visible, tangible way of conveying to others the love that God has for you. You can't do anything good enough to be loved by God *more.* You can't do anything bad enough to be loved by God *less.* If you're a follower of Jesus, you are loved, you are in the hug, you are in the beloved. Everything God wants you to have, you have in Him. Everything God wants you to be, you can become in Him.

> *Everything God wants you to have, you have in Him. Everything God wants you to be, you can become in Him.*

Since you are greatly loved, love others greatly. Open up your heart and open up your arms and welcome others into the hug.

When the power of love is flowing through you, you are a bright light in the world around you. The next chapter shows what it means to be a loving light for Jesus wherever you are.

20

Turn on Your Love Light

I read an inspiring story about a great surgeon at the Mayo Clinic, Dr. Edward Rosenthal, who is now retired. When he was eleven years old, Edward and his family lived on a farm in rural Minnesota. One day Edward's older brother became seriously ill. As they waited for the doctor to come out from the city, Edward's parents feared the worst.

When the doctor finally arrived, the whole family gathered around while he examined the very sick boy. Edward saw the black cloud of worry and concern on his parents' faces. When the doctor finished the exam, he announced, "You people can relax. Your boy is going to be fine." At that moment Edward witnessed a dramatic change in his mom and dad. Their faces were totally transformed. He could literally see the light of hope on their faces dispelling the darkness of worry and fear. That's the moment young Edward decided to become a doctor because he wanted to bring light to people's faces just as that doctor did.

You know what? The power of the love of God in your life is even better than a doctor bringing good news. I mean, when it dawned on you for the first time that God loves you just the way you are, didn't that good news light up your heart like a huge fireworks display? Isn't your life brighter every day knowing that God loves you completely in spite of your mistakes and sins?

Our whole world needs more light today. People need the light of your love, joy and laughter as a child of God. They need to know someone like you who is in love with Jesus and who is excited about life regardless of the problems you face, the trials you endure, and the defeats you suffer. The God who has accepted you in the beloved calls you to let the light of His love shine through you to everyone around you so that their lives are touched and encouraged.

Living to light up your world with the power of love is a great way to live. Bringing the light of God's love to people's lives is way more fulfilling than living to achieve great success or to see how much stuff you can accumulate. True significance comes from embracing the light of God's love personally and then letting that light shine into the dark world around you.

❖

True significance comes from embracing the light of God's love personally and then letting that light shine into the dark world around you.

❖

I want to challenge you to become a lamplighter. Now we don't have lamplighters anymore because electricity put them out of work about 100 years ago. But back in the old days, the town lamplighter had a big and important job. Every day at dusk, he carried his ladder and lantern up and down the streets of town. He would stop at each lamppost, climb his ladder, and light the street lamp from his lantern until they were all lit. After a while the lamplighter would be out of sight, but you could always see where he had been by the trail of the light he left behind.

What does it take to be a lamplighter to light up your world with the power of love? I want to encourage you with five things about sharing the light that will help you brighten up the world around you.

1. Being a Lamplighter Is a Lifetime Calling

If you are a Christian, you are a lamplighter. Your calling is to share the light of Jesus Christ every day of your life wherever you go. In John 8:12, Jesus says, "I am the light of the world." Then in Matthew 5:14, He says to His followers, "You are the light of the world." In other words, Jesus is the ultimate Lamplighter and we are His representatives in the world. We get our light from Him and take that light into the world.

What does it mean to be a lifetime lamplighter? Just look at the Apostle Paul. Next to Jesus, Paul is number one in my lamplighter's hall of fame. Check out these highlights of his life and you'll see what I mean.

Paul was a great sinner. Paul didn't start out as a lamplighter. He was just the opposite – a light destroyer. His life's purpose was to stamp out the light of the gospel. He persecuted Christians, put them in jail, and had them killed. Even Paul called himself the chief of sinners (1 Timothy 1:15). If you knew him back then, you would probably say that Paul was the last man on earth you would expect to become a follower of Jesus. Here's the point: *If God can turn a great sinner like Paul into a lamplighter, He can do the same for you no matter how dark your past has been.*

Paul was converted. Acts 9 tells the story of what happened when the world's greatest sinner met the world's greatest Light. He cried out, "Who are you, Lord...What do you want me to do?" (vv.5-6). His life was radically transformed. Later he would write, "If anyone is in Christ, he is a new creation; old things have passed away; behold, all things have become new" (2 Corinthians 5:17). When Paul met Jesus, he became a new man with a new life, new passions, new priorities, new direction, new purpose and a new agenda. He was never the same person again. That's true conversion. Now understand how I mean this – but God didn't save Paul just so he would stop "raising hell." He saved Paul – and you and me – so we would start "raising heaven." He brought us into the light to be His light in the world.

Paul was discipled. The Bible says that Paul spent years being discipled by mature Christians and growing in the faith. Later he wrote to Timothy, "The things that you have heard from me among many witnesses, commit these to faithful men who will be able to teach others also" (2 Timothy 2:2). In other words, discipleship is standard operating procedure for all lamplighters. You need to be taught and encouraged by others so you can teach and encourage others who can teach and encourage others who can teach and encourage others! Being disciples and making disciples is how we keep our lights burning brightly.

Paul was busy. Paul started serving Jesus and building the kingdom of God. He planted churches, led hundreds of people to Jesus, and wrote two-thirds of the New Testament. He impacted the entire Roman Empire in his time and the whole world since then through his preaching, teaching and writing. It's time for us to get busy spreading the light, too. Maybe for you that means starting a Bible study at school or work, volunteering at a crisis pregnancy center, signing up for a short-term mission trip or delivering meals to shut-ins. Paul was a tentmaker by trade, but his real "business" was the work of lighting up the world for Christ.

Paul was focused. He lived his life for an audience of One. He was not out to please the religious establishment or his family or his friends. His focus was to please one person only: Jesus Christ. If you live to please only Jesus, you will be a light to every other person in your life – parents, spouse, kids, teachers, supervisor, employees, everybody you meet.

Paul was fearless. He wrote, "I can do all things through Christ who strengthens me" (Philippians 4:13). He lived with a can-do spirit. His approach to ministry was "fear nothing, try anything – always in trouble, but never alone!" You know, you can spend your whole life doubting your worth, second-guessing your abilities, regretting your mistakes, and accomplishing very little. I think Paul's advice to you would be clear: "Get over it and get out there! Show up and make a play!" God can use you no matter who you are. So suck it up, live with confidence, and accomplish much for God.

Paul was humbled. He said, "A thorn in the flesh was given to me…lest I be exalted above measure" (2 Corinthians 12:7). Apparently he had a tendency to become proud, so God let something happen to Paul – a weakness or health issue of some kind – to remind him that "it's not about him, it's about Jesus." I believe that the most effective lamplighters are the ones with the greatest weaknesses, because weaknesses tend to keep us humble. If you feel humbled by your weaknesses, that's just where God wants you to be because He can use your weaknesses to make you stronger and display His strength.

Paul finished well. Tradition tells us that soldiers led Paul out of the city of Rome, placed him on a wooden block beside the road, pulled out a sword and beheaded him. You may say, "That doesn't sound like finishing well!" But you have to look at what he said before the blade fell: "I am already being poured out as a drink offering, and the time of my departure is at hand. I have fought the good fight, I have finished the race, I have kept the faith" (2 Timothy 4:6-7). It's not how many years you live; it's how you live those many years that really counts. The way you die is important, but the way you live is everything. Paul went the distance and gave all he had to become all

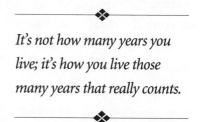

It's not how many years you live; it's how you live those many years that really counts.

he could be. By the time his lantern was snuffed out, he had enlisted a legion of lamplighters that has grown into a vast army today. When it comes to sharing the light through a person's life, you can't find a better example than Paul.

2. The Light Must Come from the Inside Out

You have to receive the light in order to give the light. You have to be connected to something that is powerful enough to shine through you. The only light that radiates the love of God is Jesus Christ. Jesus says, "I am the light of the world. He who follows Me shall not walk in darkness, but have the light of life" (John 8:12). The Gospel of John opens by introducing Jesus this way: "In Him was life, and the life was the light of men. And the light shines in the darkness" (John 1:4-5). In order to get out of the darkness and live in the light you must have Jesus Christ within as your source of light.

When I was in youth ministry, I devised a game for impressing this truth on kids. I called it "The Candle Game." The kids really loved it. I'd bring the students into the church fellowship hall, seat them on the floor and assign each one a number from one to ten. Then I turned off all the lights. With the room in pitch black darkness, I recited John 1:1-4. The key line is, "That life was the light of men." The moment I said the word "light," I struck a match and lit a candle I was holding in my hand. The kids would go, "Ooh, that's cool!" I made the point that when Jesus came 2,000 years ago, the world was dark and He was the only light in the darkness. Then the game would begin.

The object of the game was for each kid to get a lighted candle. But in order to get candles the students had to learn the "code." I was the only person in the room who had candles and knew the code. So as everyone sat quietly in the darkness, I pulled one student aside and secretly told him the code. When that student recited the code back to me from memory, I gave him a candle and lit it from mine. Then that student and I each picked another student in the room, taught him or her the code, and gave away another lighted candle.

At certain points in the game eerie music began to play and everyone had to freeze in their tracks. The music signaled that the death angel was about to speak. The kids loved this part! One of my assistants playing the death angel said in a creepy voice, "The church bus was involved in a terrible crash on the way home from camp and all the sixes were killed. If you are a six and don't have a lighted candle, you must proceed to hell." So all the sixes in the room got up and went to hell.

Well, hell for us was usually the kitchen next to the fellowship hall. Before the game we turned on the ovens in the kitchen and left the oven doors open so the room got really hot. I had a bunch of people in the kitchen dressed up like demons ready to "torment" those sent to hell. At first the kids thought "going to hell" was going to be exciting, but as the game went on, they got nervous because of all the scary noise they heard coming from the kitchen, screaming and groaning and wailing!

Then the death angel said, "But if you are a six and have a candle, you may proceed to heaven." Heaven was a nice, comfortable room with pleasant music and lots of "angels" to take care of the new arrivals.

As the death angel made surprise visits during the game, the kids realized, "Man, I've got to get a candle!" But there was nothing they could do about it until someone who had a candle told them the code. The code was three verses they had to memorize and recite: Romans 3:23, "For all have sinned and fall short of the glory of God" – Romans 6:23, "For the wages of sin is death, but the gift of God is eternal life in Christ Jesus our Lord" – Romans 10:13, "For whoever calls on the name of the Lord shall be saved."

After a while – trust me – they got the idea. They wanted to get a candle and start sharing the code with other students before the death angel showed up again. And when the eerie music started, you could hear them say, "Oh no, I'm out of time!" Sometimes the death angel said, "The entire youth group got trapped in a burning building." Then after a pause the voice continued, "But everybody got out safely and has another chance to get the light or share the light." You should just hear the sighs of relief!

At the end of the game, heaven was full of kids with candles, so the room was alive and bright. The kids in heaven spontaneously started singing praise songs. They knew they ended up in a better place. They were thankful that someone shared the light with them. But hell was a totally different experience. It was dark, hot and creepy. Some kids freaked out when the death angel called their number and sent them to hell. They were scared, some of them were crying, and some of them wanted to call their parents to come get them.

The Candle Game was just a game, but it was a vivid picture of life. There really is a heaven and there really is a hell. You've got to have the light to escape hell, to get into heaven, and to share the light with others. Your life must be anchored to something that holds you up and holds you together through all the hard stuff life brings. And the only light that can do that is Jesus. You must have the Light!

3. The Light Changes You

The light of Jesus on the inside will change you and change how you see yourself. The light always exposes our frailties, weaknesses and imperfections. Have you ever looked at your face when the lights around the mirror are really bright? The light shows up everything on your face – little bumps, wrinkles, acne scars, aging spots. If you haven't looked at yourself under a bright light for a while, you probably don't realize what you really look like. Personally, I try to stay away from those magnifying mirrors.

The bright light of Jesus shining from inside me reveals that there is nothing very special about me. Compared to the brightness of Jesus, I don't have any reason to get proud or haughty about what I am and have. The light is humbling. We tend to see ourselves based on where we are in the pecking order. If someone makes more money or has a higher position in the company, we see them as more valuable than we are. But the light helps me realize that I am no worse and no better than anyone else.

What people accomplish and accumulate in life is only secondary at best. As the Candle Game illustrated to those students, the only thing that matters in the end is that people have the Light. In the game, kids who were popular in school, talented, or from well-off families sat on the floor next to geeks and kids from the poorer neighborhoods. But if you didn't have a candle when your number came up, you were toast no matter who you were or what you had. We need the light so we can see ourselves the way God sees us.

The light should also change how other people see you. When people look at you, they should see the light of God's love shining through your face. They ought to see a smile because nothing lights up a room like a smiling face. The King James Bible sometimes uses the word "countenance" for a person's face. I always get hung up trying to say "countenance." I usually give it six or seven syllables when it finally comes out. It's like the word "hamburger" for me. For some reason it's hard for me to say "hamburger." I've been eating cheeseburgers all my life because hamburger is just too hard to say.

Countenance is the outward expression of an inward reality. Abraham's wife Sarah was "a woman of beautiful countenance" (Genesis 12:11), meaning she was beautiful inside and out. God asked Cain, "Why has your countenance fallen?" (Genesis 4:6). Cain was angry and jealous of his brother Abel, and it showed on his face. Psalm 89:15 describes God's people, "They walk, O Lord, in the light of Your countenance." God is light and so is His countenance. And because we have the Light of the world inside us, the light should show on our faces, too. For some people it's just obvious that they have the Light inside. If you are excited about living in God's love and light, people will read all about it on your face. Even if you don't say a word, people should wonder what's up with you because you're always smiling.

4. The Light Should Shine in What You Say

When I was in the sixth grade, my teacher Miss McCray gave us a writing assignment. We had to write a paper about our dreams. Well, that was easy for me. I wrote about my dreams of becoming the greatest quarterback who ever lived, playing in the NFL and making it into the Pro Football Hall of Fame. Now if you knew me back in the sixth grade and read my paper, you might have said to yourself, "Nice dream, kid, but it's never going to happen for you." I was skinny as a post. Plus, I was already a fluent stutterer. Yet, when I got my paper back from Miss McCray, she had written on it in red ink, "Neal, I believe you can do it!" Those positive words from my teacher made a deep impact on me and stoked the dream in my heart.

The light should pour out of us in everything we say. Colossians 4:6 says, "Let your speech always be with grace." We ought to say something positive to everyone we meet because our positive, encouraging words can turn a dark countenance bright. Mark Twain said, "I can live for two months on a good compliment." You never know when the positive, uplifting comments you speak will help turn someone's bad day into a good day.

In his book *See You at the Top*, Zig Ziglar tells about his early struggles. He wasn't doing anything with his life and wasn't going anywhere. Then during a conference he attended, a big-time sales trainer walked up to him and said, "Zig, you could be one of the all-time greats if you just believed in yourself." Ziglar says it was that statement by that man at that time that changed his life forever. Today, Zig Ziglar enjoys a reputation of being one of the most sought-after and highly respected speakers, motivators and authors in history! That's the power of a positive word.

5. The Light Gets Rid of the Darkness

There's no question, no doubt and no debate about what light can do in a dark room. If you walk into a totally dark room and flip on the light switch, the darkness is gone. Instantly. One moment it's pitch black and you can't see a thing; the next moment you can see everything. It's never a contest between light and dark. The darkness never says, "This time I'm going to try harder to keep the room dark when they flip the switch." If the circuitry all works and there are good bulbs in the appliances, light always defeats darkness. It's the same with the light of Jesus – wherever you take it, it will always dispel the darkness.

Author Robert Fulghum tells the story of attending a two-week summer session at the institute founded by Greek philosopher Alexander Papaderos. At the end of the session Papaderos stood up before the students and said, "Are there any questions?" No one said anything, so Fulghum asked, "Dr. Papaderos, what is the meaning of life?" There was some laughter, but Papaderos said, "I will answer your question." He pulled out of his pocket a very small, round mirror about the size of a quarter, and told this story.

He grew up in a poor family on the Nazi-occupied island of Crete. One day he found the broken pieces of a mirror from a German motorcycle that had been wrecked. He took the largest piece he could find and scratched it on a rock until it was round and smooth. The mirror became his toy and he enjoyed reflecting light into dark, remote places the sun couldn't reach. He found it intriguing.

As he became a man, Papaderos realized that his toy mirror had helped him realize that his life was only a small mirror that could reflect light into the dark places of this world and the shadowy places in the hearts of men. In answering Fulghum's question, he said reflecting light and dispelling darkness was the meaning of life. He then took his mirror, caught the bright rays of the sun coming through the window, and reflected them onto Fulghum's face.[4]

That's how we are to live our lives. We are to catch the light, let it shine *on* us, and then let it shine *from* us. I pray that you will live your life as a bearer and sharer of the transforming light of Jesus Christ. In the game of life between light and darkness, light always wins.

I have only one more word to share with you, and it may be the most important word in the whole book.

---

4 From Robert Fulghum, *It Was on Fire When I Lay down on It* (New York, NY: Ivy Books, 1991), pp.171-175.

The Last Word

It became known as the "Ice Bowl." It was the 1967 NFL Championship Game between the Dallas Cowboys and the Green Bay Packers played on the frozen tundra of Lambeau Field in Green Bay, Wisconsin. It remains the coldest NFL game on record. The field was frozen solid. The temperature at game time was minus 13 degrees, and the wind chill dipped to minus 48! Seven players suffered frostbite during the game. It was so cold that the officials couldn't use their whistles because the metal instantly froze to their lips.

Well, it turned out to be an incredible game despite the horrendous conditions. The Packers led early 14-0, but the Cowboys edged ahead 17-14 with a touchdown on the first play of the fourth quarter. They held that lead with fifteen seconds left in the game. But Green Bay had the ball on the Cowboys' one-yard line. There was time for only one last play.

In his book *Instant Replay*, Packers' Hall of Fame guard Jerry Kramer tells what was going through his head during that last huddle. He was silently praying that quarterback Bart Starr would call a play away from his side of the line. He couldn't feel his fingers or toes. He was totally exhausted. He had nothing left in his tank to make the key block on Cowboy tackle Jethro Pugh to win the game. But sure enough, Starr called a quarterback sneak behind Kramer and the center. If the play failed, the game and the championship would be lost. Kramer felt totally overwhelmed.

When the Packers broke the huddle, Jerry Kramer could hear the chant all around him getting louder and louder. More than 50,000 faithful, frozen Packer fans were screaming in unison: "GO! GO! GO! GO! GO!" Kramer writes that the relentless chant fired up something deep inside him that he had never felt before: *You can do it! You can throw that key block! You're the man! Go! Go! Go!* Dropping into his stance on the line of scrimmage, eyeball to eyeball with big Jethro across the line, Kramer reached deep into a well of resolve inside him that he never knew he had. The ball was snapped. Kramer crashed into Jethro Pugh and made the crucial block. Starr followed his big guard across the goal line and the Packers won the championship. For Kramer the winning play was ignited by the fans urging him to *Go!*

So the last word I want to leave with you is *Go!* God loves you unconditionally and has great plans for your life, and He wants you to go for it. He wants you to go higher, swifter and stronger in every area of life. He wants you to become that person He created you to be. Satan and all of his demons may try to stop you, chanting "No! No! No!" before you make a play, but all your loved ones and fans on the sidelines and in heaven are cheering "Go! Go! Go!"

I pray that by now you are convinced that every single day of your life is precious and overflowing with possibilities. Now *GO!* Make the most of every day God gives you – beginning today.

I pray that you are inspired to pursue your deepest dreams and live out God's great plans for your life. Now *GO!* It's time to get out of the boat and experience the miracles God can do through you.

I pray that you have a new perspective on the difficulties and defeats in life, viewing them as gifts to help you grow and mature. Now *GO!* Let God transform your weakness into strength.

I pray that you are fired up to believe like never before. Now *GO!* Show up and make a play to demonstrate your power of belief. Banish the word "quit" from your vocabulary.

I pray that you are humbled and blessed to find yourself "in the beloved," locked in the heavenly hug of God's unconditional love. Now *GO!* Unleash the power of that hug among family members, friends, classmates, coworkers and neighbors.

Yes, my last word for you is simply – go. Today. Don't wait until you've got things all neat and tidy. Begin where you are right now. Step out in faith and believe – trust God to do great things in your life today, tomorrow, next week, next month, next year and for the rest of your life. That's what I've done and you can do it, too. There's nothing all that special about my story, but what I have shared with you about Christ working in and through me is *real*. Whether you're a mom, a dad, a student, a business owner, a teacher, a day laborer, single, married, healthy, sick, rich, poor, young or old – my message for you is this: If I can, y-y-you can!

Go!

Discussion Guide

This guide is designed to use with groups of men, women and students – separately or mixed – as well as for personal study. If used with a group, designate someone to lead the discussion, perhaps rotating leaders from chapter to chapter. Be sure to emphasize participation, sharing of personal experiences, and practical application. If time is limited, choose in advance certain questions on which to focus discussion, and encourage participants to cover the others privately.

INTRODUCTION – Fired Up!

1. As we consider "elevating our game," what would you consider to be some right motives for elevating *your* personal game? What would be some wrong motives? Share your thoughts.
2. Football for me was a passion, and stuttering was a giant obstacle. But thankfully, God's calling on my life was greater. Do you have a passion that tops your greatest natural aspirations and obstacles? If so, what is it?
3. Read and discuss Romans 8:26-27. How does the Holy Spirit help us when we "stutter" our prayers to the Father?
4. Now read the next verse, Romans 8:28, and consider what God is saying to us in the various elements of this scripture. Discuss it a word at a time.
5. Complete this thought: "The big idea for me in this chapter is . . . ."

Prayer: *Father, take my abilities, my desires and my delights and make them always pleasing in your sight. I dedicate them fully to you. In Jesus' name, Amen.*

Chapter 1 – Life Comes with a "Use By" Date

1. If you had only one year to live, how would you allocate your energy and passion? Would it be spread out over a lot of things or a few things? Discuss.
2. If you could restart your career or life-work, what might you do differently?
3. If there are some opportunities you have missed, how would you approach them now if you had a chance to do things over?
4. It has been said that "most people never realize their full potential in life—it is buried with them." Considering the Matthew 25:13-40 passage, what is a gift or talent that you might have "buried" that could be put to good use?
5. Complete this thought: "I believe I can make an impact for good right now by . . . ."

Prayer: *Father, I don't know how long I will live, but I do know this: I want to live every single day with passion and purpose. I am determined that my life must count for something big! In Jesus' name. Amen.*

Chapter 2 – Every Time Can Be the Best Time

1. Who are some key people who have enriched your life? Some of them may be gone, some still alive. What would you want to say to them?
2. Read Job 14:1-5 and think about the fact that God has assigned us a specific number of days in this world. Make a list of positive marks you'd like to leave on the people you are able to touch in the time allotted to you. What will you do now to start making a greater contribution to people's lives?
3. Someday, someone is going to speak about the impact of your life. What characteristics and accomplishments would you like them to remember about you?
4. Complete this thought: "If I really understand that God's grace has wiped my slate clean, my mind and emotions will be . . . ."

Prayer: *Father, help me to live honestly and openly in all of my relationships. Grant me wisdom, discernment and strength to build a legacy that will bless others. In Jesus' name, Amen.*

Chapter 3 – Just One Thing

1. Review Colossians 1:15-18 to see how crystal clear God's ONE thing really is. What do you consider the "one thing" that is making or will make your life on earth truly count?
2. What does it mean for you to make Jesus Christ Lord of all aspects of your life and activity? What facets of your life do you need to focus on as you bring your whole self under His Lordship?
3. How do you define success, and what does your definition say about the priorities in your life? Who are some of the most "successful" people you have known, and why do you think they succeeded?
4. Complete this thought: "The image I want to have of myself at the end of my life's work and journey is . . . ."

Prayer: *Father, help me to become centered on Jesus Christ and His Kingdom. Help me not to lose focus or stray from the central calling and purpose of my life. Grant me the passion and energy of your Holy Spirit to stay focused. In Jesus' name, Amen.*

Chapter 4 – Everything Starts with a Dream

1. Reflect for a moment on someone whose personal dreams were contagious and motivated you to pursue your own dreams. What was it about them that challenged you to accomplish your aspirations?
2. Read Genesis 37. How did young Joseph handle his dreams? Discuss how this might apply to you as you seek to be the "steward" of the hopes and dreams God lays on your heart and mind?
3. It's one thing to think big and have lofty dreams; it's another thing to see them come true. What are the necessary ingredients that make the difference?
4. Complete this thought: "Some of my dreams are so big, only God can make them happen. For example . . . ."

Prayer: *Father, help me to know the difference between the dreams You give me and those that come from my own mind and emotions. Help me know how to confirm my dreams and aspirations by Your Word. Give me the staying power to pursue the dreams You give me all the way to fulfillment. In Jesus' name, Amen.*

Chapter 5 – Get Out of the Boat

1. Based on what you know about your personal talents and skills, what are some of the things you believe God can accomplish through your life?
2. What are some of the limitations or handicaps that may be keeping you from stepping out of the "boat"? Discuss times you've seen people move out into impossible circumstances or turbulent situations and succeed. What were the factors in their success?
3. What motivated you to "get out of the boat" and trust Christ as your Savior? Were you influenced by someone in particular? If so, who?
4. Read 1 Samuel 17. What were some of the natural fears that could have kept David from going forward to take on Goliath? What enabled him to be victorious?
5. Complete this statement: "I know that faith is stronger than fear, so I will exercise my faith by . . . ."

Prayer: *Father, may I always recognize Your voice when You call me out on the water. Help me to be so focused on You that I will not sink in fear and anxiety. Give me the boldness to step out every time You call. In Jesus' name, Amen.*

Chapter 6 – Learning to Walk on Water

1. There were times when I thought I was in over my head because of my stuttering, particularly in preaching and public speaking. What are some things God might be wanting you to do that make you feel like you're in over your head?

2. My comfort zone was that place where my stuttering wasn't exposed to others. But to move forward, I had to step out of my comfort zone. Describe some activities or situations that seem to pull you out of your comfort zone.

3. Read John 20:19-29, that describes Thomas's "whoa" moment. Describe a "whoa" moment in your experience or that of someone close to you when you or that person wanted to shout, "Whoa! You *are* the Son of God!"

4. Complete this thought: "I can say an enthusiastic 'Whoa!' when . . . ."

Prayer: *Father, give me the discernment to see when I'm crawling back into my comfort zone, and the courage to come out. Bring me those wonderful moments when You are so real in my life that I say, "Whoa! You are the Son of God!" In Jesus' name, Amen.*

Chapter 7 – You're Being Watched

1. Are you ever aware of anybody watching you? Why do you think they are watching you and what effect does this have on you?

2. Are you conscious that you are building your legacy right now as others are watching you? Who are the significant people in your life for whom you are conscious of building a legacy you can be proud of? How does this affect the way you live?

3. Read John 4:7-38 and discuss the elements that made Jesus' witnessing to the woman at the well so effective.

4. What expectations should parents have and try to enforce regarding their teens attending church regularly? How best can parents motivate their children when it comes to participating in church life?

5. Complete this thought: "What motivates me most about being involved in church is . . . ."

Prayer: *Father, I really want to impact people's lives for You and the Kingdom. Give me the strength to live alongside people every day in a way that will point them to You. Help me always to be ready to give a reason for the "hope that is in me, with gentleness and reverence." In Jesus' name, Amen.*

Chapter 8 – Comeback Wins Are the Greatest

1. Are there any lids that seem to be keeping you from reaching your potential? What changes in attitude do you need to make regarding your lids?
2. Read 2 Corinthians 12:1-10, and discuss how Paul's "thorn" became a means of growth. Describe a negative force, condition or circumstance in your past that turned out to be a positive force in your development and growth.
3. Had it not been for my stuttering, I might not have understood how much I had to depend on God. What is something in your life that seems to be an "enemy" that might actually be a "friend" in disguise?
4. Complete this thought: "I may not can control every negative thing that comes my way, but I can control my . . . ."

Prayer: *Father, forgive me for complaining about the negatives in my life rather than acknowledging them as a means of growing stronger. Thank You for Your promise to work all things together for good if I fit my life into your purpose and plan. In Jesus' name, Amen.*

Chapter 9 – Finding the Best in the Worst

1. What are some serious barriers to a positive attitude you've had to deal with – financial strain, the economy, health issues, work, relationships, business stress, home life?
2. What advice would you give a friend for navigating the murky waters of negative attitudes in order to stay positive and afloat?
3. What are some examples of hard stuff you've had to deal with, and how have you handled them successfully?
4. Read and discuss 2 Corinthians 11:23-30. What do you think some of the factors were that helped Paul keep going in the face of many challenges and difficulties?

5. Complete this thought: "Giving advice to others is not all that hard; what's hard is . . . ."

Prayer: *Father, help me to walk as a person of courage and hope in a world that is hopeless and frightened. I am claiming overcoming strength and a joyful outlook through Your Holy Spirit, regardless of what comes my way. In Jesus' name, Amen.*

Chapter 10 – God Can Use Anybody

1. Think for a moment of some of the people who have been in your corner, encouraging you and cheering you on in life. If you're in a group, share together.
2. Reflect on some of the big challenges you are facing right now and how your personal attitude is going to be a factor in overcoming them.
3. How do you respond or react when you feel you have done the right thing, but the situation only gets worse?
4. Read and discuss Matthew 10:26 and 2 Timothy 1:8. Are you aware of any projects or responsibilities you are facing that cause you to be anxious and fearful. What should your attitude be toward them based on the Scriptures?
5. Complete this thought: I have been reminded in this chapter that I can view the difficulties and scars in life not simply as weights and hindrances, but as . . . ."

Prayer: *Father, thank you for the scary things in life that have driven me into Your strong arms and enlarged my faith in You. Give me the confidence to press on even when I falter and feel afraid. In Jesus' name, Amen.*

Chapter 11 – Someone Wants to Take You Down

1. Read John 10:10. Do you think Satan has stolen anything from you? If so, what actions will you take to get it back?
2. List some things in your life that may make you a "target" for the adversary, and what you must do to get rid of them.
3. Why do you think God allows the enemy to attack and tempt you in the first place? What does 1 Corinthians 10:13 have to say about this?

4. Describe your understanding of being sifted. Has there ever been a time in your life when you think you have been sifted? Share with the group?
5. Complete this thought: "The next time I'm faced with the possibility of being sifted, I'm going to ...."

Prayer: *Father, I thank You for sending Your Son into the world to give me a full and meaningful life. Make me aware of any weak areas where Satan is likely to attack me and try steal that abundant life away from me. I am claiming Your presence and strength as protection. In Jesus' name, Amen.*

Chapter 12 – Fatal Flaws

1. Based on what you have read in this chapter, when does a flaw in a person's character becomes "fatal"? In your opinion, what are some of the warning signs that a fatal flaw is in process?
2. Consider any flaws in your life that you may be doing battle with that can potentially ruin your Christian influence, wreck your relationships and keep you from God's best in life. Share together.
3. What are some action steps for dealing successfully with any flaws that could potentially become fatal?
4. Read 2 Timothy 4:10. Find a Bible dictionary or commentary and read about Demas. What do you think it means when Paul writes that Demas had "deserted because of loving this present world"?
5. Complete this thought: "I know that simply being aware of my sins and flaws is not enough. I must ...."

Prayer: *Father, I praise You that through confession and commitment my flaws are sanded down, smoothed out and taken away. Now lead me into relationships with people who will support me and help me grow stronger in my faith, so that I, in turn, can support others the same way. In Jesus' name, Amen.*

Chapter 13 – It's Never Wrong to Do the Right Thing

1. What are some of the pressures or forces at work today that are causing our people and culture to slide into accepting "wrong" things as "right"?
2. Describe a person you've known and admired who has a reputation of spotless integrity.
3. What are some little things people do that can eventually grow into big things that bring them down? Habits, business practices, unhealthy relationships, compromising situations, etc.?
4. Read and discuss Romans 7:14-25. How does Paul's struggle reflect your own struggle? How do you deal with the temptation to do what is wrong when in your heart you want to do what is right?
5. Complete this thought: "When I am faced with the choice to compromise my convictions and do what I know to be wrong, I will . . . ."

Prayer: *Father, guide me so that I will not step blindly into the quicksand of wrong choices while society stands by and watches me sink. Protect me and warn me for what lies ahead so that when I am confronted with the choice between what is right and wrong, I will always choose what is right. In Jesus' name, Amen.*

Chapter 14 – I Believe

1. Consider for a moment your personal core beliefs that have brought spiritual transformation to your life, a greater sense of purpose and peace of mind. If you are in a group, share together.
2. Who are some individuals you know or have known whose personal character and behavior have inspired you to seek a closer walk with Christ?
3. Read and discuss Matthew 10:13-17. Why would "belief" come before "understanding" – as Anselm of Canterbury taught?
4. Read Ephesians 4:1-3. Is there a gap between your belief and your actions? How are the two related and what do you need to do to close the gap?
5. Complete this thought: "I want my belief in Christ and my personal walk with Him to be anchored . . . ."

Prayer: *Father, strengthen me at the core of my being. I want to be a person of depth and substance who cannot be lured away from faith into doubt or unbelief. I want to be able to distinguish clearly between what is good and bad, and what is right and wrong. In Jesus' name, Amen.*

Chapter 15 – Make a Play

1. Are you dealing with any situations right now that are challenging you to "make a play"? If so, describe them. Consider their urgency and what might be hindering you from moving forward.
2. The kind of plays we are talking about have a way of revealing our true beliefs and level of commitment. How will your beliefs be clearly seen through the plays you need to make?
3. Begin with Genesis 3:9 and move through your Bible, noting some characters who made great plays for God. Note the significant impact they had on history.
4. Complete this thought: "The single biggest play I need to make right now is . . . because . . . ."

Prayer: *Father, I want to be a first-string play-maker for You! I ask for discernment to spot the opportunities that are screaming out for attention or resolution, the wisdom to know the right thing to do, and the courage to do it. In Jesus' name, Amen.*

Chapter 16 – I'm Still Here!

1. When you think of the word "champion," who are some personalities that immediately come to mind?
2. What characteristics do you think enable the true champion to emerge and rise to the top?
3. During the rise of Hitler and World War II, German theologian and pastor Dietrich Bonhoeffer wrote in his book *The Cost of Discipleship,* "When Christ calls a man, He bids him come and die." In contrast, what is the modern culture's attitude toward making costly commitments, particularly those of a spiritual nature?
4. Read Daniel 1 and discuss how Daniel was placed under tremendous

pressure in Babylon. What were some of his secrets for enduring and persevering through difficult circumstances? How did Daniel's behavior in Babylon enable him to function as a champion for God in that land?

5. Complete this thought: "In my own strength, I cannot ... but I promise. ..."

Prayer: *Father, thank You for Jesus, my personal Champion and the ultimate Champion of all mankind. I am determined to move forward in Your strength and power to be a champion for Christ in the "Babylon" where I live. In Jesus' name, Amen.*

Chapter 17 – Honk, if You Believe

1. Take a moment to summarize the "gospel according to a goose."
2. Why is it important to have the right people around you? What are some character traits they should possess? Who are some of the right people in your life?
3. Are you currently involved in any projects, school organizations or causes that are bigger than you are, that challenge you to step up and pay a price in time and commitment? Describe what you can contribute personally to make these projects successful.
4. Who has God placed in your life that needs your encouragement? What do they need to hear from you, and how will you come through for them?
5. Read and discuss Philippians 3:1-14 and 2 Timothy 4:7, then complete this thought: "I know that temptations will come and Satan will try to keep me from finishing the race, but ...."

Prayer: *Father, thank You for the people in my life who have shown true leadership and have stirred a desire in me to be a leader who can help others run their race in life and win. I want to finish strong with confidence and satisfaction just like the Apostle Paul. In Jesus' name, Amen.*

Chapter 18 – A Love that Can't Be Stopped

1. What does God's "unconditional love" mean to you personally? Describe a time and situation when you experienced His unconditional love?
2. If you are a parent or plan one day to be a parent, you probably have a

vision of how you want your children to turn out. Discuss some of the aspirations and dreams you have for your kids.

3. Now read and discuss Jeremiah 1:4-5 and Psalm 139:13-16. What potential do you think God saw in you before you were formed in your mother's womb that you now have a chance to realize?

4. Do you really believe God chose you for Himself? Why do you think He chose you and invited you to receive His gift of salvation? Read John 15:16 and discuss it together.

5. Complete this thought: "The reality of God's unconditional love and plan for my life has . . . ."

Prayer: *Father, thank You for putting me in the world for a purpose, and thank You for designing me for the unique calling and mission You've placed on my life. I want to rise to every occasion and bring to the table the very best I have to offer – because of You. In Jesus' name, Amen.*

Chapter 19 – Plug into the Hug

1. Summarize in your own words what it means to be "accepted in the beloved" and to live every day "in the hug." What difference would it make in your lifestyle if you lived daily in the awareness of this truth?

2. Think of some specific people you need to pull into the hug. How can you pull them in? Who can you recruit to join you in the effort?

3. Read Acts 15:37-39 and 2 Timothy 4:11 and discuss what happened between Paul and Mark. What was going on here? Was there ever a moment when you made a huge mistake, but someone acted in grace and gave you special encouragement? Can you think of someone in your circle of friends and family who may have failed miserably and needs your hug? How will you draw them in and encourage them?

4. Complete this thought: "If I am going to reflect God's love through my life in tangible, visible ways, I am going to have to . . . ."

Prayer: *Father, thank You for loving me and believing in me even when I have messed up. Thank You for sending people to reach out to me and restore me. I, too, want to be a person who extends the hug of love and encouragement to others. In Jesus' name, Amen.*

Chapter 20 – Turn on Your Love Light

1. How do you think people develop an awareness of their true significance?
2. Before the availability of electricity, towns had lamplighters. What equipment did the lamplighter need, and how does this illustrate what we need today to be spiritual lamplighters?
3. The benefits of light are obvious and numerous. Consider for a moment what light enables you to do that darkness does not. When the light of God's love, forgiveness and salvation is turned on in a person's life, what really happens?
4. Read and discuss Psalm 18:28, 112:4, 139:12, and John 1:1-5. In the spiritual sense, why does light banish darkness but darkness not banish light? What does this suggest about Jesus Christ—the Light of the world—and His impact on our lives and the world around us?
5. Read Exodus 34:29 and 2 Corinthians 3:18 and complete this thought: When I am walking obediently with the Lord, I feel like His light is . . . ."

Prayer: *Father, I want to reflect the light of Your glory to others. I want You to be the "lamp unto my feet and light unto my path" and help me to walk and live in Your presence so that my character and lifestyle reveal Your nature. I want to be a lamplighter in a dark world. In Jesus' name, Amen.*

The Last Word

1. Does the word "go" have any special meaning to you in the context of your life right now? If so, what?
2. Is anything keeping you from "going"? Anything whispering in your ear, "Stay – don't move forward – be satisfied with things undone, unanswered and unresolved – settle for mediocrity – you can't amount to much anyway" – when in your heart you know better and sense God's voice telling you to "go"? What's holding you back?
3. Complete this thought: "Regardless of the voices that come at me casting doubt, worry, uncertainty and limitations, I'm going to listen to The Voice – that is telling me that I must give all I've got to become all I can be. So I'm going to get up and . . . !"

Prayer: *Father, thank You for the Truth of Your Word, for what I have felt, and for a fresh vision of what You can do in and through my life. I truly want to make a difference and cut a clear swathe for good and for God every single day that I live. I believe with all my heart that "I can" – therefore, "I am" going to go all the way with You – to become all that I can be! In Jesus' name, Amen.*